BOSSTROLOGY

Also by Adèle Lang

Confessions of a Sociopathic Social Climber

How to Spot a Bastard by His Star Sign
(with Susi Rajah)

BOSSTROLOGY

The Twelve Bastard Bosses of the Zodiac

Adèle Lang and
Andrew Masterson

THOMAS DUNNE BOOKS

St. Martin's Griffin ⚭ New York

THOMAS DUNNE BOOKS.
An imprint of St. Martin's Press.

www.stmartins.com

ISBN 0-312-30968-6

First published in Australia by Pan MacMillan in 1997

First U.S. Edition: January 2003

10 9 8 7 6 5 4 3 2 1

For Susi Rajah, Sahm Keily, Jane Burridge, and Alison Urquhart
for being there from the beginning.
And for little Ellroy, who tried so hard.

✪ CONTENTS ✪

✪ ACKNOWLEDGMENTS ✪

Big thanks to Jane Burridge, Anne Dewe, Thomas Dunne, and everyone else involved in bringing our work into fruition thus securing us enormous royalty checks. It's been a pleasure doing business.

Even bigger thanks to those who were hell to work for, or with, and thus inspired us to write this little tome. They know who they are. But, just in case they don't, we advise them to keep reading.

Special thanks to Sahm Keily, Susi Rajah, and Carin Siegfried for their ongoing support, advice, and encouragement during all the hard work.

Even specialler thanks to Destiny's Child: without them, Mariah Carey would have copped a real pasting here.

✿ FOREWARNED ✿

What makes all bosses such bastards? Were they deprived of Mozart in the womb? Locked up in cupboards by surly nannies? Beaten up by dorm monitors at boarding school?

No. Sorry. Bosses didn't evolve into bastards by dint of their sad, pathetic upbringing. Nor were they gradually corrupted through ever-increasing promotions and salary caps. Their unsavory ways were preordained by the movement of the stars under which, at the time, their parents were busily bonking with no thought to the misery their actions would later inflict upon the working class. Bosses were *born* bastards.

That seemingly benign little seed who made his mother throw up for nine months? Cancer boss in the making.

That cute little tyke who used to piss in your pocket when you picked him up? Gemini boss just waiting to happen.

That revolting swat who always knew the answers to the algebra test but would shield his work with his arms? Virgo boss written all over him.

And what about that teenage hooligan who stole your peanut butter sandwich and then told you it was for your own good and if you didn't stop whining or if you dared blab, you'd end up swinging from a peg in the cloakroom? An Aries boss-to-be on his first day's work experience at your office.

Bosstrology will tell you all you need to know about your employers but wish you never did: after all, you didn't really *need* to be reminded of their errant ways, since you spend 36 hours a week (minimum) in living hell with them. But at least by reading this astrologically incorrect guide you can have a laugh at their expenses—particularly since you've charged *Bosstrology* to the office supplies account, under Reference Books.

You can use *Bosstrology* to discover what makes bastard bosses tick, and how you can best wind them up. Then you can apply what you've learned and work your own way to the top. Or, failing that, at least to first in line in the unemployment line.

Of course, our in-depth and incisive analysis of bastard bosses and our expert advice on how to put one over them in the future probably won't help you right now. It won't make up for the lousy pay, the lack of recognition, or that shockingly brief and formal reference which seems to follow you to the Unemployment Office time and time again.

If it helps any, real astrologers fervently believe bosses are only human: they have kids and mortgages and interfering in-laws. They get hemorrhoids. They cry at funerals. In other words, they have feelings too.

Don't kid yourself. The only nice boss is a laid-off boss.

P.S. To all our current and future employers: nothing contained in this book is heartfelt; we only did it for the money.
P.P.S. You tight scummy bastards.

BOSSTROLOGY

THE
BOW-WHEN-YOU-SPEAK-TO-US
FIRE SIGNS

ARIES, LEO, SAGITTARIUS

Recent surveys suggest that more and more people are choos-ing to leave the workplace voluntarily. Women in their thou-sands are fleeing from middle management positions and deliberately having children. Real men in their droves are risk-ing ridicule by downing picks, shovels and Valium in order to watch daytime soaps. Even laboratory rats are organizing elabo-rate escape plans by volunteering to go first in deadly shampoo tests and then applying to undertake law degrees.

There is a very simple explanation for all of this. It's called a *fire sign*. Which, more often than not, makes it a *boss*. Because, as a rule of thumb, you have to be a complete and utter ball-tearing, egotistical, insensitive prick to get the top job in the first place.

The essential problem for hapless and harried employees is that Fire Sign bosses take their title too literally, turning it into their job description as well. They all believe it's their birth-right to nag, bully and lord it over anyone who's earning less than them.

Fire Sign bosses are easy to spot. In fact, you'll be able to hear them stomping at a brisk pace down the corridor in their jackboots, issuing orders at the top of their voices. The minions following close behind will be one of two kinds: no-brain numb-skulls, because they won't answer back; or slavering sycophants, because all the honest, straight-talking employees have been sacked. Or have left in favor of experiencing 36 hours *natural* labor. Or honestly believe that feigning an addiction to sleep-ing tablets in order to justify watching *The Young and The Restless* is far better than pretending to enjoy working for a total bastard.

THE ARIES BASTARD BOSS

March 21–April 20

You, along with the rest of your colleagues, are huddled under your desk, the only one in the office surrounded by sandbags. The Prozac has settled in nicely, the chamomile tea bags are on emergency stand-by, and some whales are warbling reassuringly through your Walkman. For a few blissful moments, you actually start to relax. Indeed, your hands seem to have stopped shaking long enough for you to contemplate picking up a pen and partaking in a little light paperwork.

That's when it happens. Again.

A door slams, a window shatters and a short fuse explodes. Unrepeatable words whistle down the corridors, followed by ground-to-air missiles masquerading as staplers, wastepaper baskets and a fifteen-thousand-dollar photocopier. *And they all land in the general whereabouts of your work station.*

Fortified by the tea bags that *you* supplied, and taking the rest of *your* Prozac with them, your so-called brothers-in-arms bolt for more protective cover, via the air-conditioning vent, and through the secret tunnel that *you've* spent the last six months painstakingly digging using a couple of unfurled paper clips. Sadly, you are forced to stay put since you don't have time to file down the industrial-strength steel chain that attaches your ankle to the leg of your desk.

And so a ballistic bastard boss comes storming toward you, and you alone, mustache bristling, eyes bulging, waggling a flimsy white square thing in a manner so singularly terrifying you will probably never be able to look at an $8\frac{1}{2} \times 11$ piece of paper in the same benign and trusting way again.

Oh, shit. It's your holiday application form. You'd forgotten about that.

Having worked for 365 back-breaking, nerve-racking days in a row, you had, surprisingly enough, thought it quite reasonable to request a weekend off to engage in a quick nervous breakdown, a rapid rehabilitation program and an incredibly speedy recovery.

As always, your Aries boss disagrees. Loudly. And with a lot of what a defense lawyer in the military would term *physical gesturing.*

"*Where's your sense of duty?*" you're asked, while being hauled out from under your makeshift bunker by the nostrils.

"*Where's your dedication?*" you're quizzed as you and your desk ricochet off well-worn walls, a completely rooted photocopier and a bewildered maintenance person who'd just come in to water the plants.

"And what's all this New Age garbage about a so-called mental illness? Don't you know that it's all in your bloody head?" your Aries employer bellows, giving you a whopping great thump in it to prove a point.

To add insult to injury upon injury, you are then told to *grow a backbone.* Easier said than done, you think (though daren't say out loud), given that your current one is being violently sanded back as you're dragged along the heavy-duty nylon carpet, desk following in agonizingly slow pursuit, toward your Aries employer's office.

Due to stringent publishing censorship laws, we're not allowed to give a blow-by-blow account of what happens next. However, we can say that the tensest moment involves a copper pot, a Bunsen burner and a small rat, and that the bloodcurdling screams to follow can be readily heard throughout the office, up to and including the air-conditioning vents.

Cut to several hours later, after you've raided the first-aid kit—only to find it's run out of Band-Aids, Alka-Seltzers and Ben-Gay—and dragged yourself and your decidedly clingy desk back to your place of work. Your Aries bastard boss bursts out of the executive den waving another white square thing. Of course, you immediately think it's the worker's accident compensation claim you've just submitted. All at once, what's left of your teeth start to chatter more than usual (your office is always freezing, the boss keeping the air-conditioning at a constant minus 37 degrees, after reading that warm temperatures slow down staff productivity), and, in an extremely amateurish but nonetheless totally sincere attempt to avoid a fate worse than death, you try hanging yourself from the chain attached to your leg.

As it happens, your mercurial boss is actually clutching a white flag, and is here to invite you for a conciliatory cup of coffee in the staff mess. As part of the truce, he's even willing to unshackle you from your desk, albeit temporarily. While self-reflection is not in any Aries employer's vocabulary—along with most other words in the English language containing more than four letters and one syllable—none of them like to think their employees think badly of them.

Naturally, this sudden *détente* places you in a dilemma: Your psychiatrist recently advised you to cut down on caffeine because it plays havoc with your nervous system. However, if you don't sup from the congenial cup, you're likely to be accused of being churlish, mean-spirited and *hostile*.

What Amnesty International, the Red Cross and Rush Limbaugh would all rate as crimes against humanity, your Aries bastard boss will decree mere crimes of passion. *"Sorry, old thing. Things got a bit out of hand back there, didn't they? But we're both adults, aren't we? Let's forgive and forget, shall we?"* Having wisely learned such questions are not actually meant to be answered, at least not in a truthful way, you do your best impression of an ace UN mediator refusing to kowtow to the unreasonable demands of an African fascist regime and nod furiously. Really, you have no choice, not unless you want to cop another barrage. And besides, you want your boss to stop shaking your hand, the one that's just been hastily wrapped with a couple of tea towels since the bandages, plaster of paris and finger splints were also missing from the first-aid box.

When you're under an Aries thumb, it's not work. It's war. The sort of war that renders you stuck behind enemy lines in a labor camp run by a psychotic Vietnam vet who saw *Platoon* one too many times as a youngster. What you call a 15-minute lunch-break, your Aries employer calls *death by firing squad.* What you call leaving the office of an evening, your boss calls *going AWOL* and doles out the appropriate disciplinary action, which also happens to be death by firing squad, though this time, without the last request. *(NB: It is no small coincidence that prospective dicta-tors of small nations use Aries-run corporations as prototypes. Nor is it a random twist of fate that most Aries bastard bosses were, or indeed still are, volunteers with the Army Reserve.)*

Aries bastard bosses don't get to high-ranking positions through privileged connections or gratuitous ass-licking. Oh, no. They steamroll, bulldoze and bludgeon their way to the top with all the subtlety and grace of an armored tank set on auto-matic pilot. And once they've acquired a taste for demolishing the opposition, they're not about to stop. No matter that the office accountant keeps telling them staff turnover is appallingly high.

Make no mistake. Aries employers like a committed worker, which is what they usually get within a relatively short period of time. Find yourself under the employ of one of these slave-drivers and you'll start actively lobbying two of your nearest and dearest to sign you away for a bit of R&R in a maximum security psychiatric ward. You'd even take it out of your annual leave, if you were ever allowed some. Unfortunately, your nearest and dearest aren't talking to you at the moment because they feel you've been neglecting them for the past 365 days. Which, to be fair to them, is quite correct insofar as you're not allowed to place social calls during working hours.

But for all your tireless efforts, you will never, ever be able to pacify your boss. All Aries employers work under the assumption that *if they want something done properly, they should have done it themselves.* For once, at least, you silently agree. It would have saved you three sleepless nights researching, writing up and then hand-binding a 72-page document for tomorrow's marketing meeting. It would also have prevented the public flogging currently being staged in the staff mess because your current Aries boss has spotted a speck of blood on page 12. *"Can't you be trusted to do anything right?"*

While your document is being used as a lethal weapon, you console yourself with the thought that at least you won't have to drink that dratted cup of coffee since it was knocked flying about the same time you were.

After venting the executive spleen and rupturing yours, your boss will glance at the clock, realize it's been at least 15 minutes since you were last seen at your desk, and tell you in no uncertain terms to get back to it. And, *"by the way, why are you lying on the floor in a bloodied heap like that? Don't you know you've got work to do?"*

How to Get a Raise.

Getting a raise out of your Aries bastard boss is relatively easy. Ask for one. That should be enough to send your employer through the roof and you through the nearby office partitioning. *"Hasn't it been made clear enough? You're not worth it, no matter what that quack shrink the company has employed says. You're goddamned lucky you've got a job."* Face it, a less lenient boss would have you out on your ear rather than hold you by it because you've had the gall to ask for more money.

How to Get a Promotion.

There are no promotions to be had in an Aries organization, only *de*motions. From your employer's point of view, *you're a good-for-nothing useless waste of space who isn't fit to lick the latrines clean.* (Which is what you've currently been assigned to do, after your worker's compensation accident claim was finally acknowledged.) The closest you'll get to rising through the ranks is when you're winched up by the scruff of your neck during the routine early morning office drill for mentioning the pay raise again.

How to Get the Bastard's Job.

If you manage to overthrow this unholy terror, you've certainly earned your stripes. However, it takes more than one plucky employee to oust an Aries bastard boss. In fact, you'll probably need to stage a coup. And something tells us you're not going to be able to rouse the troops while they categorically refuse to leave the air-conditioning shaft. At least not until the Prozac runs out.

THE LEO BASTARD BOSS

July 24–August 23

Unlike the other 11 bastard bosses of the zodiac, Leo employers are even-handed, fair-minded, generous to a fault, helpful at all times, kindness personified and a great bunch to work for. Unlike the other 11 bastard bosses of the zodiac, Leo employers are even-handed, fair-minded, generous to a fault, helpful at all times, kindness personified and a great bunch to work for. Unlike the other 11 bastard bosses of the zodiac, Leo employers are even-handed, fair-minded, generous to a fault, helpful at all times, kindness personified and a great bunch to work for . . .

It will pay you approximately $18,000 to $35,000 per annum to remember this. Indeed, err on the safe side, and make it your early morning mantra and your late night catechism. (Don't worry about remembering it during working hours; your Leo boss will be sure to jog your memory during mid-morning and early afternoon mass.) Keep thinking how privileged you are to be toiling all hours for and on behalf of this divine entity and you'll certainly hold onto your job long enough to convince your bank manager to give you that housing loan you so desperately want.

Because, woe betide any doubting Thomases, Terrys, Tanyas and Tabithas. Let so much as a single independent thought wiggle its way into your mind—a thought like, *Why am I saying something that patently isn't true?*—and you'll be out on your ear quicker than you can reply to yourself, *Because I want that bloody loan.* And to think! With a little more pandering and a lot less pondering, you'll soon be the proud owner of a three-bedroom brick-and-tile home with ensuite bathroom, games room and built-in robes.

The relationship between employees and Leo bastard bosses is not unlike that between bug-eyed, gob-smacked acolytes and Sun Yi Moon, L. Ron Hubbard, the Pope or any other crackpot religious leader. Of course, in a religious sect, you'd be made to flog flowers at airports, hand out questionnaires in shopping malls or drive ridiculous bulletproof golf-carts round Rome. Under the supreme guidance of a Leo bastard boss, you'll be assigned far less important tasks, like carrying the executive sedan chair, cleaning the wall-to-wall mirrors in the executive office, and sticking your hands together in prayer and/or applause whenever the Grand Poo-Bah enters the building. But that's okay. Unlike the suckers who decide to join dodgy cults, you're doing this for money, not love. Despite what you say to the boss.

There is a protocol that must be observed at all costs in a Leoled organization. It's kind of like a mutual admiration society, one in which the both of you agree to mutually admire the boss—"How do I love thee? Let me count the ways," or "Let there be Leo," or "Mr. Hubbard would be really *proud* of you, if he wasn't dead," or something along the same lines. It doesn't matter how insincere you are while saying this, or how ridiculous spouting Shakespeare, the Bible or *Dianetics* sounds in a twentieth-century office, your Leo boss will always, *always* believe you mean it. And you do. Sort of. You spent all night rehearsing one false compliment after another because you've now got a mortgage to pay. (Besides, this is the only job you've had thus far where you're actively encouraged to turn up in tracksuit and sneakers, with unkempt hair and makeup *au naturelle*, so you don't outshine Oh Heavenly One.)

You'd think, wouldn't you, that someone so ostensibly smart as a boss would start getting suspicious about all the nodding, smiley heads milling around the office? But nope. Your Leo boss will smugly misinterpret it as job satisfaction *en masse*.

Unfortunately, Leo bosses truly believe they're omniscient, omnipresent and omnipotent. In less enlightened times, people got locked up for thinking they were the Messiah. However, in today's world, particularly in businesses based on self-deceit or self-conceit (advertising, political parties, religious organizations, to name but a few), they tend to get the top job. And, in a way, you've only got yourself to blame. Purely for financial gain, you have inadvertently created Frankenstein's monster (albeit a much better-looking one), admired the Emperor's new clothes (beautifully cut, we might add), and sold your soul to the Devil (a really nice one, of course).

Dare to question your blind faith and your Leo boss will damn you with labels like non-believer or, sin of sins, a heathen with a lot of personal problems to work through. In other words, *you're just jealous.*

And, you being a reasonable type, will be apt to agree. You'd love an office that takes up the entire top floor of the building. You'd love to waft into work-in-progress meetings with a coterie of bodyguards, hair-stylists, makeup artists, personal priests, publicists and lighting technicians trotting behind at a respectful distance. You'd also love to have the confidence to immediately think that when an employee says "Sign this," it's a request for an autograph.

Like all living legends, when they're not puffing their chests out and banging on about their brilliant corporate takeovers, or the time they got visited by a vision of God on a mountain top, Leo employers will occasionally let you speak and provide you with counsel. This would, perhaps, qualify as a redeeming feature except it tends to run along the lines of: "Yes, that reminds me of the time when I lost my spouse, children and dog in a horrific gardening accident" (you just told your boss that your boyfriend has dropped you), or "Let me tell you about the time I won the Nobel Peace Prize" (you just told your boss you won "Secretary of the Year").

All this posturing and preening makes you wonder how the hell Leo bosses get any work done. Quite. They don't. They hire you to do it for them, then take credit for all your brilliant ideas. When the international media hails them personally for some grand business plan that *you* devised, Leo employers will graciously smile and refuse to set reporters straight, partly because self-delusion is one of their strong points, but mostly because they're dying to have their picture taken.

Bosses by definition will steal your thunder. Leo employers, however, will take it one step farther and claim they *invented* it. When you rush to your encyclopedia and point out that, at best, climatic variances did, and, at worst, God did, a Leo will look at you and say: "Your point?"

You will feel obliged, mortgage be damned, to refer to the encyclopedia again, and point to the bit about the solar system that says the world revolves around the sun, not you-know-who.

Your Leo bastard boss will then haul you into the executive chambers, sit you down on the prayer mat in front of the gold-leaf pulpit, climb up the spiral staircase that winds its way to the cloud above, and accuse you of trying to lord it over him or her. You in turn will take compulsory worker's cap off head, put it in hand, and deny all charges without once blinking. The boss will then think that, because you appear to be staring for longer than is polite, you fancy him or her. This is fine, as a Leo likes to be genuinely admired.

How to Get a Raise.

Start by knocking tentatively on the only door in the office building with a big spangly silver star hanging from it. Meekly shuffle in, and, if you can manage it without giggling uncontrollably, affect a little bow or, preferably, a sweeping one. Present your boss with a little gift as a token of your appreciation. Make sure it's tasteful, thoughtful and not too ostentatious— you don't want your employer to think it's a *bribe*. A limited edition Mont Blanc pen, a Norman Rockwell lithograph or a Rolex watch should be more than adequate.

The outrageous lies that will then issue forth from your mouth should segue nicely into asking for more money. For instance: *"God, I can't actually believe I'm standing here in the same room, breathing the same air as such an esteemed person like yourself. Can I have a 20 percent pay rise, please?"*

Whether or not you get one is beside the point. Through gross insincerity and unforgivable sycophancy, you'll be guaranteed to keep your job for at least one more monthly mortgage payment.

How to Get a Promotion.

Act dull. Appear dim. Affect Tourette's Syndrome. Fake a limp. Further ensure that everybody dislikes and fears you intensely by pretending your mother is a feminist and your father is a tax inspector. Top off your massive unpopularity by engineering a disfiguring industrial accident that leaves you looking like the Elephant Man's slightly uglier sibling. Your Leo boss will immediately single you out for promotion since you won't be perceived as a threat.

Of course, should pride, vanity or plain old common sense prevail, you can always further your career simply by quitting.

How to Get the Bastard's Job.

While your Leo bastard boss is still swanning down the corridors, parting seas and receiving wholesale worship, you've got about as much chance of getting your hands on the number one job as a pig farmer has of becoming a Rabbi. However, when your boss leaves to take on the recently vacated position of Head Leader Chairman Executive of the World, he or she will present it to you in the same manner as one would present a charitable donation. This, in turn, will make you feel exactly like you did when you were a mere employee, but at least this time around, now that you'll definitely be able to meet your mortgage payments, you'll be in a position to state, for once truthfully, "God, you're a bastard."

THE SAGITTARIUS BASTARD BOSS

November 23–December 21

History does not record the identity of the person who first con-
cocted the bizarre idea that a business would operate more
profitably if all its employees were forced, from time to time, to
leave their homes and families, trek *en masse* to some stretch of
inhospitable and leech-infested wilderness, tie ropes around
their arses, and collectively hurl themselves off a cliff in reckless
vertical pursuit of a nebulous form of enlightenment known as
team spirit.

There is no doubt, however, that it was a Sagittarius bastard
boss.

Nero, we should point out here, was a Sagittarian, and the

words *Sagittarius* and *sage* quite possibly have the same Latin derivation. This is purely coincidental, the result of some random freak of etymology. But try telling that to a Sagittarius bastard boss as he or she comes bounding through the front door, depressingly early and hideously aglow with energy and inspiration, tosses the green wax-cotton shooting jacket over one muscular shoulder, and announces: "Hey, guys, I've got a great idea!"

Time speeds up, out of control, pushed by the boss's disgustingly aerobic enthusiasm. Before you know it you're standing in a distant scrag-end copse, dressed in camouflage gear while Derek, the irritating and acne-pitted geek from the computer room, fires yellow paint-balls at you from a black and evil submachine gun which, you can't help noticing between the splats and stings, would look much better inserted barrel-first up your employer's bum.

Whether they be heading up a multinational corporation or a village shoe shop, Sagittarius bastard bosses believe in a robust and hearty assault on business. They are hands-on types, leading from the front, with a red-blooded approach to each day which would do Hannibal proud, but makes the rest of us sick to the stomach. "*Carpe diem!*" they cry, leaving everyone else in the office to wonder what the hell fish have got to do with it.

The best thing that can be said about Sagittarius bastard bosses is that they will never ask you to do anything they haven't done themselves. This is good, except that they have done absolutely *everything*—or so they'll tell you—*and* enjoyed the challenges encountered along the way, however dangerous.

Which brings us to the worst thing that can be said about Sagittarius bastard bosses: they will *frequently* ask you to do things you neither care nor want to do yourself. Such as orienteering on a wet weekend. Or bronco busting. Or sky-diving. These activities build *character*, the boss will proclaim, and an employee with *character* is more effective than one without.

Point out that an employee with *both legs in working order* is more effective than one without, and you will be reminded forcefully of Mohammad Ali. What would *he* be doing today if he had not taken risks in life?

Probably not dribbling and twitching uncontrollably, you think, but keep your mouth shut.

Persist, and point out that the connection between jumping out of a moving aircraft and doing your job, which consists primarily of answering the telephone, seems, well, rather tenuous, and you will be informed, with impressive authority, that a *quitter never wins, and a winner never quits.*

"There is no room for *passengers* in this business," the boss will caution. This perhaps explains the proposal to push you out of the Cessna in mid-air instead of letting you stay inside it until it lands again.

"Every problem is an *opportunity*," he or she will then add.

Suggest that this is the first time you have ever come across the concept of a life-threatening opportunity, and you will be told, ominously, to *consider your position.*

You, of course, have been doing that throughout the conversation. Your current position is seated on a well-upholstered hydraulic chair in an air-conditioned and carpeted office. It seems infinitely preferable to the position being advocated by the boss: spread-eagled and plummeting 3,000 meters above a rapidly approaching field full of cow shit, 140 kilometers from your loved ones.

Yosemite Sam was probably a Sagittarius. Also Foghorn Leghorn. Also Gomez Addams.

There is one job to which Sagittarius bastard bosses are superbly suited, allowing full expression of their natural abilities to combine leadership, physical exercise, travel and mind-numbing platitudes. Unfortunately, there are simply not enough cruise liners in the world to keep one-twelfth of the world's population employed as recreation officers.

The rest of them, therefore and sadly, have been forced to take up positions in other industries. Destiny, however, will not be denied, and the globe is full of Sagittarian builders, bankers, gardeners, garage owners, stockbrokers, spies, sports commentators, restaurateurs, rodeo riders, pimps, publishers, party-planners, engineers, ear-nose-and-throat specialists, speculators, spatula manufacturers, milliners, miners and motion picture makers who approach their businesses and employees with all the painful bonhomie and bullying needed to organize a jolly game of desk quoits between port and starboard passengers somewhere west of the Azores.

NB: There has never been a Sagittarian nun. Except possibly Saint

Radegunde (518—587 AD), a woman who felt that the best way to build a united team and convert the European pagans to Christianity was to brutally demolish and burn their shrines. (A dead giveaway, this. She probably called it motivational bonding.)

It is a little known fact, but in many countries Sagittarians are actually banned from positions of power and influence in certain industries. Prime among these is diplomacy. Contrary to popular belief, most wars throughout history were not started by ruthless and unhinged dictators trying to annex a neighboring country. They were started by Sagittarian diplomats on goodwill missions.

Ditto life-saving. It is a sad reality (and one stubbornly unacknowledged by Saggies) that nine out of ten drowning people do not appreciate being told to, *kick, dammit, kick! You'll never get anywhere in life if you just flail about like that!*

On the other hand, though, there are a number of responsible positions into which Sagittarians are positively encouraged. This is partly because only Sagittarians manage to combine the bluff good humor, rude good health and mindless jabbering such positions require. Partly, too, it's because no one else is stupid enough to take them on.

These jobs include:

* devising television programs with names such as *Gladiators* and *Survivor*;
* running commando units;
* commentating at the Olympic Games;

✳   coaching girls' hockey teams in fee-paying schools; and

✳   not much else, really.

Patently, though, Sagittarians have managed to insinuate themselves into a far, far wider array of jobs and industries. In fact, recent studies indicate that as many as seven out of ten cases of employee absenteeism due to pulled muscles, sprained ankles, rope burn, extreme irritation, multiple fractures, immersion in cow dung, airsickness, and bruising caused by falling off bucking stallions are directly attributable to the boss having been born under the sign of the archer.

This is plainly one of life's great cosmic misfortunes.

How to Get a Raise.

Plan ahead. You must turn yourself into the boss's idea of a model employee. Six weeks before making your move, start jogging to and from work. Remain in your sweaty rain-soaked togs throughout the day (make sure these are of the professional, tight and brightly colored variety), because to the Sagittarian mind a good worker is a quietly putrid worker.

Play squash every lunchtime. Offer to play the boss—no true Sagittarian will be able to refuse. *Make sure you lose, preferably doing your hamstring in the process.*

Continue jogging, using crutches. And wearing hiking boots.

Say *Yo!* a lot. Rub liniment all over your body at four-hourly intervals. Subscribe to *National Geographic,* and have it delivered to the office. Become addicted to anabolic steroids.

Ask for the raise. You will receive it.

Then contact the Salvation Army. Ask them if they can track down your spouse and children, given that they haven't been home for four weeks, ever since they unsuccessfully pleaded with you to seek psychiatric help.

How to Get a Promotion.

Do not under any circumstances suggest to the boss that you would like a higher position in the company. Do so, and you will only find yourself shivering and terrified, perched on the edge of a bridge with a length of rubber tied around your ankles, unwillingly testing the boss's firmly held belief that productivity and bungee jumping are inextricably linked.

Ask, instead, for more responsibility, and, with any luck, the boss will smile, congratulate you on your initiative, deliver a jarring pat to your back, and let you carry the hockey sticks.

How to Get the Bastard's Job.

Simple. Merely inform the other staff that if they were to deliver to you their unswerving loyalty, they would no longer be expected to do anything more physical than stroll to the corner pub at 4 P.M. every Friday for a few beers and a gander at the football replay on ESPN.

Tell them to keep quiet about your plans.

Then suggest another of those fantastically motivational sky-diving weekends.

Offer to pack the boss's parachute.

THE
WHERE'S-YOUR-TIME-SHEET?
EARTH SIGNS

TAURUS, VIRGO, CAPRICORN

Working for an Earth Sign boss is a lot like working for the public service. Except you're more likely to get flexi-time, maternity leave and holidays in the public service, and you can shirk work, call in sick, and join the union too.

But, if you do like punching time clocks, enjoy eating sandwiches at your desk and can keep your social calls to an absolute minimum, you'll have a hoot of a time. Oh, and if you can stand working for someone with appalling dress sense, that's an added bonus.

These sticklers for detail, punctuality, and hard graft without the corruption, will tell you off if you so much as giggle—which you won't if they're the ones telling the joke. Promise.

Because they're usually married with kids, Earth Sign bosses don't have a sense of humor (mind you, even if they're single and childless they still won't have one). And because, more often than not, they have the mandatory mortgage to complement their domestic bliss, they've become experts at penny-pinching. At home *and* at work.

Therefore, all the office phones have long-distance blocks on them, all the lights are installed with time-saving devices and they're too mean to put sanitary bins in the girls' bathrooms. Furthermore, they tend to like to preside over corporations, companies and small businesses that have a staff to work-experience-kid ratio of roughly one to five.

Thankfully, Earth Sign bosses are incredibly easy to pick out in a large working environment. This is very handy if you've decided to put a contract out on them after they refused to renew yours, mainly because you kept insisting that Clause 5, the one banning long lunches, be deleted. They leave early at the company Christmas party to catch up on paperwork; they're never present at staff farewells in case they might have to pick up the tab; and no one ever pops into their office and asks them if they had a fun weekend because they invariably didn't.

THE TAURUS BASTARD BOSS

April 21–May 21

There are three ways of doing business: the right way, the wrong way, and the Taurus way. Sadly, for the legions condemned to toil beneath astrologically bovine bastards, only two of them bear any relationship to reality.

Every Taurus bastard boss once had a great idea. Well, an idea, anyway. And that one idea, he or she is deeply convinced, is as good now as it ever was, as many a haplessly helpful employee has found out at considerable cost. Never mind that the world has moved on. Never mind that the market for Chubby Checker albums has virtually dried up—medical science having discovered less disturbing emetics—flogging the bloody things worked well enough in 1965, and it'll bloody well work again. Just as soon as the rest of the world returns to its senses.

To suggest that the average Taurus bastard boss is obstinate is an understatement proportionally similar to concerns about hydrogen bombs having the potential to crack the plaster in the family room. Suggest to the Taurus boss your carefully planned, researched, costed and fully referenced scheme for upping company turnover by 20 percent—for instance, by selling stuff that people might actually *want*—and you'll be told that the Stubborn Sonofabitch Corporation didn't get where it is today by pandering to silly fads. Make surfboards? Piffle! Nobody will want surfboards by this time next year. Stick to making horse-drawn bathing boxes. There'll always be a market for horse-drawn bathing boxes. Just as soon as the rest of the world returns to its senses.

Actually, you won't be told anything of the sort. You will be expected to receive the rebuke telepathically. Taurus bastard bosses say what they think and think what they say. They are people of very few words. The likely response to such a sure-fire idea is a period of uncomfortable silence, broken only by the regular insertion of takeaway Chinese food into the executive gob, an unnerving, blinkless, brown-eyed stare (which the unwary sometimes interpret as contemplation, but is, in fact, the necessary facial accompaniment to the difficult act of eating and breathing at the same time), followed by the word "no."

Taurus bastard bosses, in fact, are very good at "no." It's "yes" they find tricky. To say "yes" is to admit the possibility that the decision to take out the overdraft to enable the continued retail of sharpened quills to the book trade (which, after all, worked very well in the year 1300) might have been unwise. Taurus bastard bosses don't like possibilities; they much prefer certainties. One certainty, in particular: that they are *right*. The quill market will recover. Just as soon as the rest of the world returns to its senses.

There is a better-than-average chance, therefore, that your boss is Taurean if the company is concerned with the manufacture, marketing or retailing of any of the following:

* manual typewriters
* vinyl records
* Hula hoops
* steam-driven motor vehicles
* chainmail
* wind-up clocks
* black-and-white televisions
* Beta video cassettes
* the sheet music to *Hair*
* Chairman Mao badges
* vacation packages to Kabul
* carbon paper
* barbiturates
* Fabergé jeans
* unilateral disarmament
* British beef
* God

This is not to suggest, of course, that all Taurus bastard bosses are incorrigible, uncommunicative and immobile. Not at all. Okay, yes it is. But Taurus bosses are perfectly capable of making decisions and acting upon them. It's just that they like to consider any such move carefully, slowly, and, preferably, while chewing. Entire species have become extinct during the time it takes a Taurus bastard boss to mull over the intriguing notion of opening the shop on Saturdays. Right now, somewhere, a Taurean head is slowly nodding to itself, having finally decided that roller skates might just catch on, after all.

All of which, in some ways, sounds pretty cushy from an employee's point of view. If the boss is going to stubbornly refuse to change anything, then, surely, work routines should be a doddle. Mind-numbingly dull, yes, but a doddle nevertheless.

Wrong, sucker. Although normally distant and reticent, Taurus bosses are all possessed of a temper so violent and unpredictable that Mike Tyson appears placid by comparison. This is because, deep down, every one of them is utterly convinced that he or she is the only person in the world who is *right*. (Of *course* wooden dentures are the way of the future, and, with 5,000 pairs in the warehouse, it's only a matter of time before everybody else realizes, and the company *cleans up*.)

Challenge the boss's wisdom once (*"Are you sure we should keep buying Liquid Paper, Guv? It leaves little white splodges all over my computer screen."*) and you'll cop the baleful-stare-rhythmic-chomping response. Do it again (*"But, Guv, I'm sure there wouldn't be a 'delete' button if it wasn't safe to use it. They've done tests and everything.*") and you will be told in sudden, stentorian terms that never, never, in all the boss's born days, has he or she come across a more irritating, ignorant, annoying little prick than you. You will then experience a rare physical sensation, known only to people who have had their faces forcefully inserted into a plastic tray half-full of chicken chop suey and buckwheat noodles.

The boss doesn't actually *like* chicken chop suey and buckwheat noodles, by the way. Far too bloody trendy. Much prefers a good slice of deep-fried cod and a shilling's worth of chips, wrapped in newspaper, like they used to do. It's just that no one seems to want that sort of thing anymore, not for lunch, not in the city. But they will. They will again. Yesterday's news will be big business tomorrow. Just as soon as the rest of the world returns to its senses.

How to Get a Raise.

Difficult, this, given that Taurus bastard bosses are parsimonious to a fault. The best way to go about it is to hint, rather than ask directly.

Start turning up to work on foot, shoeless and dressed in rags, day in, day out. Bring your own lunch: a slice of bread and lard, perhaps, or a simple handful of sand. Replace your desk lamp with a candle. Replace your desk with a tea chest. Put a small pigeon on it, labeled URGENT MAIL ONLY.

Before you know it—or, at least, before you reach retirement age—the boss will reward you, upping your wages because you appear to be someone after his own heart.

How to Get a Promotion.

Seeking a promotion presupposes that the boss knows what it is that you actually do. This is a foolish assumption in a Taurean work environment. To the average Taurus bastard boss there are only two positions in the business, even if that business is multinational in size: the Boss, and Everyone Else.

Requests for promotion are therefore worrying, and unsettling. They suggest unrest, change, ambition, desire, new ideas, forward motion. They are therefore unthinkable.

Abandon your efforts. Wait for someone above you to die, and then quietly assume that position. The most common cause of death among Taurean-employed workers, by the way, is asphyxiation due to windpipe blockage by chicken chop suey and buckwheat noodles.

How to Get the Bastard's Job.

Do nothing. Say nothing. Ever.

Recognizing your obvious management qualities, the Taurus bastard boss will eventually ask you to look after the business, in an acting capacity, while he or she goes off for a short vacation.

Agree, and then ask when the company can expect its leader to come back. There will follow several long moments of myopia and mastication. And then the reply: Just as soon as the rest of the world returns to its senses.

Enjoy. Make plans to redecorate the office, starting with the name on the door.

THE VIRGO BASTARD BOSS

August 24–September 23

You arrive at your work at 8:59 A.M. to find, what a surprise, a memo from the Virgo bastard boss.

Just a couple of points, it begins, beneath the mysterious legend D54/S2 May 2 **(inexplicably, your eyelids start to droop).**

RE: Acct # 348/bdu/opm5, from 4/27. Need to follow up. Quite some time now. Please do ASAP.

RE: ASC form 351A. What's the problem, here? Simple, surely.

RE: Petty cash rcpt # 25 from March (3/15) (yours) for $2.80. What? Please itemize. First asked you six weeks ago (4/10). Still waiting. **Need** to get this sorted out.

RE: Jonathan Adams/Amalgamated Textiles (4/25). Did he ever call back? If no, pls call. If yes, pls update yr phone log (important) (incoming stored in TELINMAY in EXCEL, yr subdirectory, **today** pls).

RE: Personal appearance. Watch pls. Today's (ie, yesterday's) shirt, creased at shoulder. Not good. Also, lime green unwise. Bear in mind, pls.

RE: Can't remember (now 9:25 P.M. (yesterday)). Is **important**. Pls remind me (memo me—hard copy to me (give to Sarah), hard copy copy you (file), soft copy me MEMOMAY in Word on LAN, copies to MEMOGEN and MEMOBACK ditto (you know this), back-up to floppy (also give to Susan), delete original (can't be too careful—competitors can **hack**) and memo Sally to adjust stats in DISCFREE (FILE MANAGER in WINDOWS, subdirectory INTERNAL, subdirectory MEMO, subdirectory TRAFFIC). Tnks.

RE: Check stationers: need list of Filofaxes (size, pages per diem, organization, etc) soonest. Mine is full, and still six months of yr to go. Tnks.

Have a nice day.

As always, you sigh. You haven't a clue what any of this means. You are the janitor. The one the boss calls Jerry, even though everyone else calls you, correctly, David. You have no idea who

Sarah/Susan/Sally is, but you suspect it may be a reference to Sandra, the boss's PA these past six years.

Virgo bastard bosses operate on a need-to-know basis. They don't need to know your name. That's *your* responsibility. That's what you're *paid* for.

Most bosses occasionally feel compelled to count their blessings. Not the Virgo bastard boss. The Virgo bastard boss feels compelled to *list* them. Every couple of days. With updates, addenda, errata, supplementaries and appendices.

In whatever industry they find themselves, Virgo bastard bosses cannot help but give full reign to the two obsessions which relentlessly drive them forward: record-keeping and paranoia. The first of these inevitably fuels the second, leading the boss to the unavoidable (if spectacularly incorrect) conclusion that his or her competitors are just *itching* to get their hands on the company's completely itemized and costed records of in-house coffee consumption (seasonally adjusted).

Look after the pennies and the dollars will look after themselves. Every mickle makes a muckle. If it's not on the page, it's not on the stage. These are the fundamental tenets of the Virgo business philosophy. Every little action, no matter how insignificant it seems, must be recorded, cross-referenced, verified and filed. Instantly and with razor sharp concentration.

Want to know the precise number of *With Compliments* slips used in August, 1982? The Virgo bastard boss can tell you.

Want to know who was on the phone at 4:27 P.M. last Thursday? The Virgo bastard boss can tell you.

Want to know how many milliliters of oil have been applied

to the squeaky hinge on the door to the Accounts Department since June last year? The Virgo bastard boss can tell you.

Want to know what the business actually does? The Virgo bastard boss wouldn't have a clue. But he or she could tell you *how* it does it, in excruciating and mind-numbing detail. It is no coincidence that the phrase "anal retentive god" is an anagram of "a latent Virgo need."

This obsession with petty detail may appear admirably organized, but it comes, always, at a price. Virgo bastard bosses are not Big Picture People. They are meticulously accurate and meticulously well prepared. If they knew what for, they'd be dangerous. They are, in fact impressively pointless. You know those people you sometimes find in street markets, the ones who offer to engrave your name on a grain of rice? Virgo, every one of them.

Which is why, even as they're peering through their magnifying glasses, they will often pause and glance over their shoulders. Virgo bastard bosses firmly believe that just because they *think* someone's out to get them, it doesn't mean there isn't. Virgo bastard bosses refuse to believe in a conspiracy until they can't see it.

A Virgo bastard boss opening a business meeting typically does so with the phrase: "Thank you for coming. Why are you *all* here?"

Unless, that is, the Virgo bastard boss is going through a bad patch (which happens roughly once every 48 hours). Then the opening statement will be: "Thank you all for coming. Why are you staring at me?"

Virgo bastard bosses can crop up in a wide range of commercial areas, but are particularly attracted to those which involve a hell of a lot of record keeping. They make excellent Head Librarians (able to quote the Dewey Decimal number for *A Year In Provence* in an instant, but have to ask directions to the toilet), statisticians (familiar with wheat harvest figures from 1948 onward; always forget briefcase), and doctors (own every pharmaceutical index ever published; convinced suffer from every disease listed therein).

Where no records exist, however, no Virgo bastard boss will venture. The Virgo bastard boss's version of Genesis goes like this: *God created the world in six days. On the seventh he rested. On the eighth he started the paperwork. An interim report should be ready next month.*

Working beneath a Virgo bastard boss is thus a distinctly tricky task, requiring superhuman ability, boundless patience, and a resilience to criticism bordering on catatonia. This is because, despite the fact that nine gigabytes inside the company computer are groaning beneath the weight of day-to-day minutiae, there are three things that no Virgo boss ever seems to know.

These are: (1) what your name is; (2) what you do; and (3) how you are supposed to do whatever it is that you do while simultaneously recording every letter, memo, Post-it note, invoice, receipt, phone call, fax, e-mail, meeting, discussion, exchange of pleasantries, cup of tea, rubber band, car journey, elevator ride, sandwich, twitch, grin, leer, pencil purchase and pee-break involved in doing it.

You must never, however, point this out. Do so, and the Virgo bastard boss will immediately take a break from writing memo *D54/S9 May 3* [the one titled *42 Ways To Improve Your Efficiency— Please Take A Moment To Read This, Then File It (Let Me Know Where Using Standard Reply Form B56/9)*], and tell you in no uncertain terms to stop whining. After all, he or she will add, there is a business to run, and no one can be expected to know *everything*.

How to Get a Raise.

Let's face it: you *deserve* a raise. Anybody who has to put up with that much pettifogging, nit-picking, hair-splitting, trainspotting anal retentiveness deserves every shekel they can get.

Send a memo, listing in point-form at least two dozen reasons why you think you should be paid more money. It won't work, but the boss will be delighted to make six copies of it and place one in each of your personnel files, each with the notation, *"This one has ambition. Could be plotting something."*

You will then be sacked for dumb insubordination.

How to Get a Promotion.

Win the boss's respect and admiration by concocting a system guaranteed to make the already voluminous amounts of data being stored swell even more, preferably by a gargantuan degree.

If you are, for instance, the cleaner, spend a weekend constructing maps of the office, grid-referenced and color-coded according to the type, amount, volume and weight of the rubbish and dust encountered.

Suggest to the boss that these maps should be completed every day (then double-checked by a second party), and the results tabulated, printed out and circulated, month by month. Volunteer to write a summary (with at least three tables and a graph) at the end of every quarter.

Not only will you receive a posher sounding title (such as Activity By-Products Monitoring Officer), you will also be rewarded with your own computer terminal, a log book, and a stream of memos which will immediately make your little area consistently the most garbage-heavy in the building.

You will then be sacked for gross untidiness.

How to Get the Bastard's Job.

You don't *want* the boss's job. Believe us. Life is too short.

Do not, however, tell the Virgo bastard boss that. If there's one phrase the Virgo boss can't understand (apart from "I didn't get a receipt for that postage stamp"), it's "*Believe me, I'm not after your job.*"

THE CAPRICORN BASTARD BOSS

December 22–January 20

It has taken, by your count, nine weeks, but your application to see your Capricorn bastard boss has finally been approved. You are told this by Michael, the irritating dweeb Virgo manager, the guy who boasts of running the day-to-day affairs of the company and tells of *having the boss's ear.*

It's not true, of course. In reality, the Capricorn bastard boss is in full and exclusive possession of the executive hearing equipment. Indeed, if pressed, the boss could boast of *having the manager's balls.*

But at least Michael has met the boss, which is more than you can say. Then again, you've only been with the company six years, so what do you expect?

Michael leads you out of your own little office and along the corridor for your appointment with destiny. The corridor—you have never ventured down it before—grows darker and colder as you go. Your footsteps echo. You go through a door marked "Boss." Michael stays behind. It is not his turn.

Inside, the room is full of shadow. It is painted beige. There is a desk, also beige, in the middle of it. On that desk rest two files, beige, a telephone, beige, framed photographs of the boss's father, mother, grandparents and great-grandparents, all beige, a season ticket to the opera (Mozart's *The Beige Flute*), an invitation to dine with a prominent District Court judge (His Honor Justice Beige), and the keys to the Bentley (guess). Behind the desk is another patch of beige, neat, well defined, somehow, well, *beiger*, and slightly more solid than the rest. It seems to have hair, parted down the middle.

That is the boss. "Good morning," she says. "Sit down. Your name is Phil. You are a filing clerk. You are 27 years old, come March. You are married, have one child, a daughter named Melinda, and live in a two-bedroom house five miles south of here. You are paying $642 a month in mortgage to Citigroup. You drive a white El Camino, leased, not unlike the one your mother used to drive before her accident. You park it on your front lawn. Your hobbies include crosswords and hiking. You support the Miami Dolphins football team but disagree with the coaches about the talent available for quarterback. You are wearing green underwear and there is a small peanut butter smear on the right-hand side of your shirt, which is a pity because you've only owned it a week and a half. What can I do for you?"

Among other things, you were about to tell the boss you felt ignored at work. "Ah, nothing," you stammer, turn and run back through the door. You realize that you have, in fact, seen the boss many, many times before: in your own office, in the canteen, in the hallways and meeting rooms of the building. It's just that, up until now, you'd assumed she was a stain on the wallpaper.

Two days later, a memo arrives on your desk. It is from the boss, telling you that your application for a fortnight holiday next month has been confirmed. You read it and go pale. That was the other matter you were going to raise.

That's the thing about Capricorn bastard bosses: they know *everything*. Always. They hear everything. They see everything. They probably even smell everything. And yet they never talk.

At least, they never talk to *you*. And why should they? You are an employee, and therefore, by Capricornian definition, unimportant. There is no *advantage* in talking to you.

Most Capricorn bastard bosses are nicknamed "God" by their minions, but this is inaccurate. They do not imagine themselves to be God. God, they think, wastes far too much time in flashy display—all that showy plague-of-locusts stuff—and isn't nearly mysterious enough. Mind you, if a cocktail invitation from the Almighty arrived, they'd RSVP like a shot. Capricorn bastard bosses are far more concerned about *who* they know than *what* they know.

In fact, Capricorn bastard bosses don't worry at all about *what* they know, and for very good reason. They know everything.

In particular, they know this: you have to *get on* in this world. Their parents taught them that. They got it from *their* parents. Nothing else matters. The Capricorn bastard boss's ancestors were all in the same business: *prospering.* The Capricorn bastard boss deeply respects forebears. (Of course, *your* Capricorn bastard boss hasn't seen her dear mother and father in a decade. Why should she? They don't know anyone who earns more than $60,000 a year anymore.)

So where does this leave you, the employee? Out of luck for a dinner invitation, that's where.

Here is a guest list for a small soirée thrown by a Capricorn bastard boss. Pick the deliberate mistake.

* The Pope
* The Archbishop of Canterbury
* David Bowie
* Hillary Clinton
* Kate Moss
* Julia Roberts
* Benjamin Netanyahu
* Jason Seahorn and Angie Harmon
* Phil from Accounts

That is, of course, unless you happen by some accident of birth to be distantly related to Caroline Kennedy Schlossburg, in which case you might be asked to come along to help the Seahorns settle in, as long as you promise to leave before dessert.

And should this happen, you will be in the rare position to watch a Capricorn bastard boss in action. The spread will be magnificently set, with Ben, Julia, *Il Papa* and company seated just so. (You'll be crammed up the end, next to bloody David, knocking your knee against the table leg.) The shimmer of neatly coifed pale brown at the top of the table will ask the occasional question—about the Archbishop's new wallpaper, perhaps, or Kate's recipe for niçoise salad—but for the most part will remain silent, sober, immobile, impenetrable, and, above all, *listening.*

The next day, and without informing anyone (least of all you, Phil, despite your entertaining anecdote about knee reconstruction, the one that Jason found so funny he almost paid attention), the Capricorn bastard boss will solve the differences between the three great major religions, bring peace to the Middle East, prevent flooding in Pakistan, pair Hillary off with the Archbishop, get Kate a job with the United Nations, have Julia made a saint, and convince David to retire.

She will do all this, of course, not for fame or glory, nor even for the good of humankind. Not at all. She will do it because . . . well, can you *imagine* the sort of deals you can swing once you've won the Nobel Peace Prize? God would *surely* have to put her on His A-List then . . .

How to Get a Raise.

There is no need to ask for a raise. The Capricorn bastard boss already *knows* that you want one. He or she already knows, too, that you're not going to get one.

There is, however, another method, although it could take a while to pay dividends. Go and visit the boss's father in the $5000-a-week, maximum security nursing home, the one the boss put him in after the last of the Old Man's influential friends passed away. Tell him you don't care that he doesn't know anyone who drives a Porsche. Tell him you are not a Capricorn. Tell him you'll be the son or daughter he always wanted. (It doesn't matter which; the old coot's half-blind anyway.) Before you know it, tears in his rheumy eyes, he'll be calling for his lawyer and a copy of his will.

How to Get a Promotion.

Status is everything, and, in the Capricornian business empire, must be recognized. You have, therefore, two options. Send money to one of those American businesses with names like The Holy Gospel Tennessee University For Divinity Research Pty Ltd and get a hefty-sounding degree by mail order. Or you can enter one of those periodic British auctions of unwanted noble titles, the ones where you can become the Baronet of Outer Sodbury for under a grand.

Phil from Accounts doesn't have a chance. The Reverend Doctor Phil from Accounts, or Phil, Seventh Earl of Wolverhampton, from Accounts, is another matter entirely.

How to Get the Bastard's Job.

There are many methods here, but most of them involve Holy Water, cloves of garlic, incantations, thick wooden stakes and tend to be uncontrollably messy.

The best way, though, is to make use of the Capricorn bastard boss's grim determination to absorb information without comment. Request an audience. Once it is granted, sit down (try not to cross yourself too obviously), and recount in as much detail as possible the plot of *Dawson's Creek* from the first episode to the last. After a while, you will hear a popping noise. That will be the boss's head exploding.

Switch on the light. The office will be empty, except for a mysterious small pile of beige dust on the executive chair. Sweep it off and take your position. Call Michael the Virgo dweeb and tell him to get Claudia Schiffer on the line, see if she's free for lunch.

THE
WE'LL-GET-BACK-TO-YOU-
ON-THAT
AIR SIGNS

GEMINI, LIBRA, AQUARIUS

When is a boss not a boss? When the bastard's an Air Sign boss.

If you were to make terrible indecisions that cost your company millions, skip work to go and play golf, or whine to your Indian guru during office hours, you'd be fired. Air Sign bastard bosses, on the other hand, by bluff, nepotism or sheer bad luck, are made company directors.

One thing's for sure: this lot do not lead by example.

For instance, one of them will spend hours agonizing over nothing whatsoever. One of them will spend hours agonizing over decisions before never making them. And the other one will spend hours agonizing over things that have nothing to do with the tasks at hand.

It must be noted, though, that while Air Sign bosses do not good mentors make, they *do* enjoy revelling in the fruits of their protégés' labor. After all, they've got nothing better to do since you do all their work for them.

Naturally, it's very hard to take any Air Sign boss seriously. This is why, invariably, most employees are told they lack the proper respect when they are dismissed by the Managing Director's personal assistant because the employer was out sailing/shopping/meditating that day and so couldn't do it himself.

This complete lack of regard for your professional well-being makes them invaluable as referees. When your next bastard boss rings for reassurance about your employment potential, your previous Air Sign employer will either have forgotten you and so will feel compelled to give you a glowing reference (just in case you deserve one), will be too much of a fence-sitter to say anything really rotten, or will never actually be available for comment.

THE GEMINI BASTARD BOSS

May 22–June 21

You left work at five o'clock on Friday evening, tentatively clutching the elaborate flower arrangement from the foyer (one of the few perks of your current job). After a lengthy stay on an eminent psychiatrist's couch over the weekend, you arrive back at the office at nine o'clock the following Monday morning, clutching only the expensively gained knowledge that if you're mad enough to work for a Gemini bastard boss, you deserve to feel off-kilter, unstable and out of sorts.

So now, like the beginning of every other working week, you walk into the office foyer, carefully survey your surrounds and try to *spot the difference this time.*

Well, your switchboard has all but disappeared and, in its

place, there's an IBM computer complete with complex software. True, the phone doesn't seem to ring half as much as it did last week, and your paycheck appears to have increased somewhat. Only thing is, there's a note attached to it requesting that you work out everyone else's and you haven't got the faintest about tax regulations, superannuation by-laws and . . . and . . .

Hah! Got it! You're the *company accountant.*

Of course, last week, you were actually the receptionist, but your Gemini boss obviously got bored with the same face greeting him on the mornings he decided to show up for work. So now you're stuck balancing books and crunching numbers. And, no doubt, next week you'll be twiddling your thumbs and staring out of windows after you're appointed National Sales Manager—Candle Wax Division (the company doesn't actually sell candle wax; it sells nuclear arms).

The only constant things in an "organization" headed up by a Gemini are chaos, confusion and an inordinately high rate of employer absenteeism. Consummate saboteurs and experts at hit-and-run, Gemini bosses never show up for duty until the exact moment the office is running like a well-oiled machine. Only then do they come bounding in, armed with half a kilo of sugar and a siphon. After the entire corporation grinds to a sudden halt, they'll be long gone, no doubt up the road to the local Off-Track Betting outlet to place a 3:1 bet on Running Second finishing first in the fifth race at the Kentucky Derby.

However, at this point in time, you've got more important things to worry about than what your boss is up to during working hours. For instance, you've just discovered he's raided the petty cash tin, omitted to fill in his cab charge vouchers, and on his way out, decided to sack the employee of the month because he, well, felt like it.

Before you know it, you're literally wondering whether you're Arthur or Martha. This is probably just as well since your Gemini employer wouldn't have the foggiest, either.

Trifling details like names, let alone job descriptions, are meaningless to a Gemini-born boss. You are not a person, you are an object, and one only worth noticing if it comes with an interesting affliction or predilection. You are not Arthur the PR whiz and aforementioned employee of the month. You are *"that set of buck teeth with the limp that I just fired."* You are not Martha the rocket scientist. You are *"that pair of overalls with the big tits."* Or your real name is Leesa, but you are called *"that thing that's bonking those ferrety-looking towel-heads from the Middle East."*

The only items on the daily business agenda of any real interest to a Gemini bastard boss are work-based scandals—mostly because they're more fun than actual work-based *work*. While unable to recall your name or that of the company's most important client, your employer has an uncanny knack of knowing the ins and outs of a rat's backside and/or your personal life. As receptionist, you'd been so used to him not listening to you for longer than a nanosecond, you thought you could bang on for hours on the phone to your mother about your current disastrous relationship with a rodent and half the Iraqi Ba'ath Party. As it happened, your Gemini bastard boss was loitering at a nearby fax machine and, tired of deliberately deprogramming all the pre-set instant dial numbers, was actually paying attention for once in his miserable life.

Working for a Gemini bastard boss is much like trying to look after a hyperactive five-year-old who, at the same time, acts like a middle-aged madman who, at the same time, thinks he's a senior citizen suffering from Alzheimer's disease. If you're a minder in a day-care center, an orderly in an old people's home, or a warden at a lunatic asylum, you'll probably be a dab hand at coping. Unfortunately, you're more likely to be stuck in a large office, small shop or fair-to-middling nuclear arms factory, doing a pretty good impersonation of a prematurely aging young person going rapidly round the bend.

Life doesn't get any easier when your Gemini boss performs one of his numerous daily disappearing acts. Even when absent, he'll manage to make his devastating presence felt. Before he slips, sneaks, runs or waltzes out the door, he'll fail to let you know that you'll have to cut everyone's wages this month because he's dipped into company funds again. He'll also omit to tell Arthur about the press release he promised Greenpeace. And it'll completely escape his mind to mention to Martha that he promised Saddam she would whip up and deliver five rockets by Thursday next week.

If, on the rare and momentous occasion, your Gemini boss does happen to be within seeing-eye range, it's still very hard to keep his attention for too long. So, if you need to speak to him, make it snappy. Indeed, if you can narrow down your current projected accounting figures into a precis of—oh, let's see—

three or four well-chosen words, such as *huge*, *profit*, *margins* and *Iraq*, then you'll definitely rise in his estimation. Remember, also, to record any conversations in memo form, otherwise your Gemini bastard boss will immediately forget what transpired and, worse still, won't admit that he's forgotten.

For instance, say you really *were* Martha, the company's rocket scientist, and you very carefully reminded your Gemini employer that if he presses the big red button marked DON'T TOUCH, deadly radioactive molecules will invade the entire building, and all his staff will immediately start bleeding from the ears.

Within a matter of moments, you'll hear the inevitable: "*Hey, you! The one with the big tits! Why didn't you tell me that if I pressed the big red button, all my staff would immediately start bleeding from the ears?*"

When you insist that you did tell him, he'll call you a bald-faced liar (not an unfair accusation given that, thanks to the high levels of radiation currently seeping through the office, your hair is falling out at an alarming rate). Then you'll be made to pop the corpses of your colleagues into plastic trash bags all by yourself because your Gemini bastard boss can't stand the sight of blood. An unfortunate phobia, you think grimly to yourself as you start the body count, considering that the relatives of the bereaved will soon be baying for his.

Of course, Gemini employers should never be allowed to make life-or-death decisions at all. Unfortunately, they always seem to be given very responsible jobs. This is only because they are very, very good bluffers. Most of those people who manage to become doctors or lawyers without the appropriate degrees, and subsequently end up in newspaper headlines like "MY BRAYNE SURJUN GOT IT WRONG (SIC)," OR "LAWYER RIPS ME OFF," are usually Geminis.

But, even if they can't tell a brain from a kidney or a lawsuit from a linen one, Gemini bastard bosses will always put on a pretty convincing show to the contrary. Despite their acting prowess, however, you're not likely to find them on stage or screen. Probably because professional acting requires rehearsal. It requires reading a script. It requires getting into the inner psyche of a character and playing it for long enough for the audience to become familiar with what the hell is going on. Those Geminis who *do* end up in the spotlight usually do so in the capacity of game show hosts.

The only good thing about a Gemini is that when you do eventually catch him in his office, you can storm in, trash his in-tray, and rant on about his reprobate, duplicitous ways, handing in your resignation while you're at it without fear of repercussion. This is because, later that day, when your Gemini boss gets back from a quick 18-hole game of golf, he will pass you in the tea-room, have a friendly chat about the merits of plutonium versus uranium, and act like nothing ever happened. Which it didn't. Did it? Oh, okay then. In that case, you're fired.

How to Get a Raise.

After being fired, turn up to work the next day and appoint yourself National Sales Manager—Candle Wax Division. Get a copy of the standard salary and pay conditions contract. Falsify it. Take it to your boss when he gets back from placing a 3:1 bet on Running Second running first in the fifth race at the Kentucky Derby. Elated that he managed to triple company profits in less than five minutes, he won't bother looking at the fine print, or, indeed, the big print. Then leave the signed contract in the capable hands of the new company accountant (formerly the receptionist).

How to Get a Promotion.

Simple. Just assume your newly self-appointed role as *International* Sales Manager—Candle Wax Division. Your boss won't remember that you were previously just the national one. But, be warned. Your days of doing sweet fuck-all for huge amounts of money will be limited. Because, when the boss gets it into his head to reshuffle and re-jig the organization after baseball season's finished, you'll probably end up back on reception again.

How to Get the Bastard's Job.

When your Gemini bastard boss has snuck off to the board-room to watch the Yankees try to pitch a perfect game against the Braves, sneak into his office and sit in a suitably proprietor-ial manner in his swivel chair. When your boss returns three months later, affect a supercilious air, look down your specta-cles and simply say: "Yes?" Having completely forgotten that he's the boss, he'll no doubt slope off to sit at the switchboard, pissing off the new receptionist (formerly Arthur the PR whiz) no end.

THE LIBRA BASTARD BOSS

September 24–October 23

To describe a Libra bastard boss as an oxymoron is to use two more syllables than are strictly necessary.

In the competitive, cut-throat world of business there are only two ways in which a Libra finds him or herself in a position of governing power: by accident, or inheritance. Or, usually, both.

Life being the perverse thing that it is, this often means that Librans are prone to find themselves, suddenly and through no fault of their own, in charge of enormous, and enormously diversified, companies which, by their very nature, require firm, ruthless and iron-fisted control. This is, to put it mildly, unfortunate. That the great stock market crash of 1987 happened in mid-October was no coincidence.

The Libran ascent to power usually begins three genera-
tions before birth, with Great-Grandfather, a Taurus, building a
modest but sweat-soaked stake by selling, say, fruit and vegeta-
bles from a hand-pushed cart. Grandfather, an Aries, keen as
mustard and full of ideas, takes over the business and opens a
small shop.

Father, a Capricorn, in turn, takes over a business comprising
ten small supermarkets, five trucks and holdings in eight market
gardens, two wool mills, an abattoir, and a chicken farm. He
floats the company on the stock exchange, retaining a 30 percent holding, guaranteeing his family a perpetual seat on the
board of directors, which he now shares with representatives of a
retail giant, two superannuation funds and an insurance company with a nice line in inspirational television adverts.

By the time Dad retires and cedes his seat to the young
Libran (a disappointment at grammar school and university,
but a nice dresser) the company owns hypermarts in 40 cities
across three continents, an airline, the second largest fleet of
trucks, vans and container ships in the world, agricultural prop-
erties which, when combined, occupy an area slightly larger
than Botswana, two bauxite mines, a computer software company in a key client role with IBM, 15 skyscrapers, a worldwide
chain of franchised kebab restaurants, a telephone company in
South Korea, a political party in Paraguay and a small but
enthusiastic bank in the Antilles.

The sudden death of the CEO leads to a vicious boardroom
brawl, with expansionist and rationalist factions locked in an
unwinnable battle to gain control of the empire. In the face of

shareholder unrest, press speculation and the prospect of awkward questions being asked by Securities and Exchange Commissions in three countries, the board reaches an expedient compromise and elects to its head the one member who has never expressed a loyalty to either faction—mainly because no one ever bothered to ask him on the rare occasions he remembered to turn up to meetings.

Blinking in the sudden glare of media attention, and hurriedly smoothing invisible creases from his latest Armani suit (bought that morning, especially for the occasion), the newly appointed Libra bastard boss steps bravely to the fore.

And none too soon. He confronts his first major corporate dilemma only hours later . . .

LIBRA: Could I have a toasted cheese and tomato sandwich, please?

WAITRESS: American or cheddar?

LIBRA: Um . . . what's the difference?

WAITRESS: Well, they taste different, don't they? Which would you like?

LIBRA: Of course, yes. [*Long pause.*] Ah, which would you recommend?

WAITRESS: I like cheddar myself, but it's up to you.

LIBRA [*with sudden confidence*]: Cheddar, eh? Yes, cheddar then. Right.

WAITRESS: Butter on top? Salt and pepper?

LIBRA: Ahh . . . Oh, look, I'll just have a pie instead, please. And do you have a tissue? My upper lip seems to be very wet.

This, of course, will be by no means the only decision the Libra bastard boss will make in the three short months before what seasoned business editors will term "the most spectacular and unexpected corporate crash in memory."

On *Day Two* he will hurl himself into the crucial question of just how his office and boardroom should be redecorated. He will circulate a memo to all heads of department calling for ideas on color schemes, furniture and fabric, and then circulate a second memo seeking expressions of interest from those wanting to form a subcommittee to consider them.

On *Day Three*, in a move analysts will later describe as "innovative" (as in "unexpected and unbelievably stupid") he will telephone his stockbrokers and instruct them to launch a takeover bid against Georgio Armani. His brokers ask him if he's really sure he wants to do this. He says he'll get back to them about that.

On *Day Four*, the vice president (Offshore Retail, Southern Region) asks him to decide whether the terms suggested for the partial, phased divestment of the Macao hypermarket in a gradual partnership operation with the Shanghai Investment Corporation takes sufficient account of likely fluctuations in the currency market over the medium term, particularly in respect of parities and disbursements set against the significantly improved performance of the retail sector in the greater region as measured by the Hang Seng index, and whether growing concerns about the delicate political situation *vis-à-vis* Taiwan, *vis-à-vis* the Spratly Islands, and the consequent weakening of the ASEAN nations *vis-à-vis* debt-linked aid programs offered by the G7 group in the next round of GATT talks, should warrant a renegotiation of the tenancy conditions and the marginal tax rates they attract.

He says he'll get back to him about that. Then he faints.

On *Day Five* he decides to take an extended vacation in Monte Carlo. The news triggers a rapid sell-off on the stock exchange which, in turn, prompts the banks to call in their debts, effective immediately, which, again in turn, leads to employees all over the world getting their shocked and tear-stained faces on the front pages of newspapers beneath head-lines predicting (accurately, as it turns out) financial ruin for millions.

The next time anybody hears of the Libra bastard boss is when he's sighted in a Rome side street, dressed in Yves Saint Laurent leisure wear, asking passers-by what they think of the paint job on his hand-pushed cart.

How to Get a Raise.

Act quickly. Time is not your ally. Never ask for a raise directly—you'll only cause the Libra bastard boss to panic and announce he'll get back to you about that.

Instead, *remind* him that he already *agreed* to give you more money, and then, just after complimenting him on the cut of his sports jacket, present him with the contract to sign. He will do so immediately and without hesitation (or reading it), because to do anything else would be to invite the prospect of debate, negotiation, and exactly the type of firm direction to which he is constitutionally allergic.

One point here: when drawing up your contract, pay special attention to the redundancy provisions. You'll be very glad you did.

How to Get a Promotion.

Research, then lobby hard. Asking the boss is obviously a bad idea, since your carefully worded internal memo, reminding him of your years of service, your qualifications, your performance results, your loyalty, trustworthiness, popularity, energy, enthusiasm, commitment and excellent dress sense, will without doubt end up about half-way down the yard-high pile of documents neatly stacked in the tray on his desk marked *Pending*.

If the company is still in business more than 12 weeks after Libra's unwitting achievement of leadership, then, clearly, someone, somewhere, is making the necessary decisions. Your task is to find out who that person is.

The chances are it will be his secretary, who, since the nameplate changed on the big door, has daily dealt with a constant stream of department heads asking her to just sign this document, a formality really, not worth bothering His Nibs about.

By now the secretary has attained an intimate knowledge of every aspect of the company's business and prospects. Quietly and without fuss, she has invested her meager savings accordingly, and is now just days away from launching a leveraged buy-out that will see the smarmy coot and his fancy suits out on his ear, once and for all.

Discover this plan, and then quietly tell the secretary that, if she really wants to succeed, your services could prove invaluable. She will tell you to fuck off. Try another tack: threaten to blow the bid to the papers before she launches, thus driving the share prices up and, quite possibly, causing the boss to return from the tennis court before next Tuesday.

She will agree at this point, and smile at you with a funny look in her eyes that reminds you, strangely, of the look a saltwater crocodile develops when it sees a kitten in the water.

How to Get the Bastard's Job.

This is extraordinarily difficult, even assuming the company which he heads is sufficiently robust to survive his tenancy.

The standard usurping strategy of building up a power base on the board by questioning his actions simply won't work, mainly because he'll never take any.

Championing your own ideas may well find favor among your colleagues, but do not assume that the Libra bastard boss will see you as a threat and force a showdown. Quite the contrary, the Libran tendencies toward tact and diplomacy will come into play: he will smile at your audacity (in that vacant way he has) and let you get on with it. You will, in fact, make him feel *more*, not less, secure, because, clearly, you're going to get on with your schemes whatever he thinks about them. And that's good. That means you won't *ask* him what he thinks about them.

And that means, in turn, he won't have to think about thinking about them and then, thinking about them, decide what he thinks about them. Which means, he thinks, that he can stop thinking about thinking about thinking about them, or, in thinking about them, thinking about what he thinks about thinking about them (at this point he pauses, and announces he'll get back to himself about that).

There is, in fact, only one sure way to replace a Libra bastard boss in the power and influence stakes. Resign. With your payout, buy a hand-pushed cart. Work hard. And wait.

THE AQUARIUS BASTARD BOSS

January 21–February 19

There is no one more constitutionally ill-suited to being in business than an Aquarian. Aquarians detest the very idea of business, loathe the competitive urge, cannot abide exploitation, and have a deep-seated ethical problem with the concept of the profit motive. (They're none too keen on porterhouse steak, either, but that's another story.)

This means, in short, that the average Aquarian bastard boss is forever coming up with peculiar and socially responsible schemes—marketing vegan dog food, for instance (*"Not Tested On Animals"*)—and putting them into play with a degree of ruthlessness, secrecy, parsimony and savagery that would make Caligula blush. (*"Why is this little girl crying? Because her pet Dart-*

moor pony has just been flayed alive in front of her, just to feed your *dog. Feed him Parsnip-O, instead, the meat-free, dolphin-friendly alter-* *native!"*)

Somebody has to force capitalism, kicking and screaming, into the New Age, the Aquarian boss reasons, and that someone may as well be him or her.

Aquarian bosses are, well, bastards to work for. They come across as so nice, so fair, and so reasonable that the average employee daily has to fight the urge to either puke or lash out blindly, fists clenched around the cardboard tubing in which that revolting Death Valley National Park poster arrived.

For a start they reject utterly the very notion of *boss*. They see themselves more as *facilitators, motivators*, or, in extreme cases, when the Prozac supply has dried up, *catalysts for change*. They are not in the business of business, they reckon, but on a mission to improve the world, pragmatically working from *inside* the system. Any money they may make in the process is merely a side issue.

The working environment within the Aquarian corporate headquarters will show two tell-tale characteristics. First, the boss will insist that he or she is never called "the boss," or "Sir" or "Ma'am," but simply "Bill," or "Jane," or just plain "Swami, Light of Divine Understanding."

The second is the sharing of information. Aquarius bastard bosses believe that knowledge is a common resource. In practical terms this means they feel not merely disposed, but positively *obliged* to sit on the edge of your desk and drone on and on and on about the personal and philosophical dilemmas they daily face in maintaining the integrity of their spirit against the dehumanizing imperatives of commerce.

Aquarians read far and wide, seeking knowledge in obscure and darkened corners of history. Thus will the boss perch nearby, interrupting your bookkeeping, sigh, and say, *apropos* of nothing: "Oh, [insert name here], in the Second Century AD, Apuleius of Madaura wrote '*If it please you, we will assume with Aemilianus that fish are useful for making magical charms as well as for their usual purposes. But does that prove that whoever acquires fish is*, ipso facto, *a magician?*' Is it any wonder I don't sleep at night?"

He or she will then wander off, not waiting for your reply, adjusting the plaited cord belt around the chinos in the process, tweaking the Palestinian tea towel around the neck, sit at the Big Desk (the one with the miniature Zen sand garden next to the telephone) and spend the next two hours pondering the potential returns and tax-break opportunities of the Ethical Investment Trusts suggested by the broker.

The famous Aquarian conscience and idealism place marked restrictions on commercial activity. As a handy rule of thumb, there is a good chance your boss is Aquarian if the business is in any way associated with the retail, manufacture or marketing of:

* recycled paper napkins;
* hemp T-shirts;
* hemp anything elses;
* porcelain dolphins;
* pulses and pakoras;

✳ carob cakes;

✳ potato curries;

✳ any other natural laxative;

✳ isolation tanks;

✳ togetherness weekends;

✳ alpaca wool jumpers;

✳ alpacas;

✳ ostriches;

✳ worms;

✳ any other form of political candidate;

✳ Paraguayan worry dolls;

✳ Native American earrings;

✳ Balinese ceramics;

✳ Nigerian pottery;

✳ Ethiopian children;

✳ incense;

✳ frankincense;

✳ myrrh;

✳ Ecstasy, acid, cocaine, peyote buttons;

✳ any other form of fashion accessory;

✳ fennel;

✳ fungus;

✳ fake fur;

✳ philosophy;

✳ books by J.R.R. Tolkein;

✳ books on finding the Goddess within;

✳ the sequel to *The Beauty Myth*;

✳ anything else remaindered;

✳   I-Ching coins, runes and Tarot cards;
✳   compact disc recordings of waterfalls, oceans or singing
    sperm whales;
✳   herbal teas;
✳   soy milk smoothies;
✳   crystals;
✳   Buddhas;
✳   anything else that doesn't actually bleed or mew patheti-
    cally when you try to gift wrap it.

Do not assume, however, that just because on your first day
at work the boss welcomes you, insists on first name communi-
cation, inquires after the health of your chakras, gives you a
clove cigarette, throws in a quote from *The Tibetan Book of the
Dead* and offers to make you a cup of rosehip tea, that life under
an Aquarian regime will be a doddle.

Oh no. To do so is to make a fundamental error. Aquarius
bastard bosses do not see themselves as part of the capitalist system, *but victims of it.* In a perfect Aquarian world, after all, everyone would recognize that love, peace, harmony and a weekly
bout of Shiatsu would be enough for contentment. Money
would be seen as the cumbersome barrier to spiritual enlightenment that it really is.

Given, however, that the world is far from perfect, the
Aquarius bastard boss reasons that the best way to seek empow-
erment is *to beat the bastards at their own game,* thereby sticking up
a metaphorical finger to the forces of fiscal evil, and also securing the freehold on a substantial four-bedroom holiday home

(constructed entirely from recycled native hardwoods) in Woodstock.

Make no mistake, the Aquarius bastard boss is as tight as a turkey's bum on Thanksgiving. They are scrupulously honest, and would no more think of removing a paper clip from the office without due cause than murdering their own grandmothers. Therefore they assume—indeed, *insist*—that all employees observe the same protocols.

Everything in an Aquarian business is meticulously documented. Even the paper recycling bins are subject to stock-take, a necessary part of the Energy Audit undertaken each month. Leaving the light on in the toilet can be a sackable offense (the sack, at least, being preferable to the other option, which is having to listen to the jerk's interminable lecture about the earth being a fragile, finite gift borrowed from our *children*, for which the wanton waste of electricity is a greater sin than buggering a goat outside a Catholic kindergarten).

The flipside of freedom is vigilance, they reason, and the handmaiden (well, OK, handfacilitator) of vigilance is *attention to detail*. In triplicate. Ten minutes ago.

Maintaining one's ethical integrity, after all, is a serious business, and the Aquarian quest to be a Better Person In All Things can afford no interference from employees who do not share The Vision. There are dogs out there, still tragically enjoying meat. And magical fish to be pondered.

It is Important Work that they do. You would set your holiday application above all this? Shame on you.

How to Get a Raise.

You would think—wouldn't you?—that a boss so dedicated to the reform of capitalism, so apparently unconcerned with the accumulation of wealth, so committed to equality and spiritual principles, would be a push-over when it came to forking out a little extra dosh to a loyal employee.

Think again, sorry. Ask for a raise and the much-troubled brow of the Aquarius bastard boss will furrow and a long, sad sigh emit from between the sensitive lips. A billion people on this overcrowded planet are starving to death, you will be told. Does this mean nothing to you?

Giving you a raise, the explanation will proceed patiently, would jeopardize *the whole point of the exercise.* It would cut into the 0:05 percent of net profit which is donated to the World Wildlife Fund. It would endanger the weekly contributions made to sponsoring malnourished infants in Third World countries. It could delay plans to open the boss's newest venture, the Indigenous Falafel Bistro And Macrobiotic Healing Center, which the market research indicates should be returning 15 percent on investment by the end of the first 12 months.

If there's one thing an Aquarius bastard boss can't stand, it's a self-interested employee.

How to Get a Promotion.

Do nothing. Staff turnover in Aquarian businesses is high, with disgruntled employees—no longer able to stand the boss's never-ending homilies, quotes from Timothy Leary, and insistence on stocking only skinny-soy-carob-decaf-low-fat-lite in the canteen—positively lining up at the exit door.

If you can maintain an adequate supply of Valium and learn the delicate art of appearing to read *Shape* during your downtime, a better position within the organization should be yours within, oh, a week of arriving.

How to Get the Bastard's Job.

Be careful here. You may not want it, unless, of course, you happen to be an Aquarian yourself or, alternatively, capable of extraordinary feats of insincerity, conceit and the bearing of false witness (Geminis, step forward).

For all other signs, there is no point to achieving bosshood unless you can enjoy the fruits and perks thereof. This is, of course, out of the question in any business constructed by an Aquarian. Aquarius bastard bosses don't believe in perks; they believe in suffering. Aquarius bastard bosses are the only people on earth capable of getting a kick out of compassion fatigue.

If you decide to go ahead, however, we recommend waiting

until the boss is working late. Take hold of the hefty and satisfy-ingly solid lump of quartz crystal on the receptionist's desk, and employ it in a short, sharp and repetitive bludgeoning manner.

When the police make the inevitable inquiries, look nervous and whisper something conspiratorial about an anti-boss plot by the World Bank and certain pro-development factions within the government. That should throw them off the scent. Then order a new Tasmanian wilderness poster, blood stains not being the easiest things to shift.

THE
WE-KNOW-YOU'RE-OUT-TO-
GET-US
WATER SIGNS

CANCER, SCORPIO, PISCES

Anyone who can't stand being ridiculed, rejected or ripped off should never have been made boss in the first place. Yet, by some miraculous twist of fate, Water Sign bosses still exist.

Odds on, if you're constantly finding your boss sniveling behind the S-bend in the staff toilets because an employee laughed in her face over a really stupid idea, she's a Water Sign. Chances are, if you come in late one night to type up your résumé and find your boss rifling through your top drawer or reading your personal e-mail, he's a Water Sign. Likewise, if the office sweepstakes gives your boss a 100:1 chance he'll still be in charge come sundown, chances are he's a Pisces.

When they're not blubbing in bathrooms, following you around with a surveillance camera, or attending Effective Business Management seminars, Water Sign bosses are most likely to be found skulking in their offices hatching vengeful schemes in an attempt to get you before you get them.

Being such an intuitive bunch, they sense that you know you could do their job with your eyes closed, your hands tied behind your back, and your brain sitting in a jar on the bookcase across from your desk. So don't wonder what that strange crackling noise is on the end of your phone (it's being bugged). Fret not as to why your office window is currently being bricked in (you don't deserve one). And quit worrying over whether or not you'll get work in this town again (you won't).

Of course, some of the petty tricks your Water Sign bosses get up to make you wonder who exactly *is* the bloody employee here. But never point this out. They've got enough insecurities and inadequacies without you adding to them.

THE CANCER BASTARD BOSS

June 22–July 23

It is a startling fact that in the history of the world no Cancer bastard boss, from Julius Caesar onward, has ever sacked an employee (cities, yes, but not employees). Many a crab-dependent worker, however, has been *downsized, made redundant, let go, laid off, given cards, restructured, rationalized, relieved, rendered surplus, out-placed, shelved, freelanced, disengaged, despatched, disenfranchised*, and just plain *strategically reassigned onto the open labor market.*

Cancer bastard bosses are constitutionally incapable of saying what they mean. Talking to a Cancer bastard boss is very much like consulting an oracle; you have to *interpret*, and hope for the best. He or she will never, for instance, come right out

and tell you not to wear that nose-ring while serving the cus-
tomers. Oh no. You will be asked: "Are you comfortable in that
jewelery?"

Think carefully before you reply. You *need* this job.

And thinking carefully about Cancer bastard bosses is a far
from easy task. Try it some time. List everything you know about
your employer—that person you see five days a week, carefully
observed from behind the rubber plant you strategically positioned on your desk in the vain hope that you'd be mistaken for
an aphid and left alone.

Chances are, you'll come up with this:

* Talks funny
* Moody bugger
* errr . . .

And that'll be it. Waste of a perfectly good Post-it note.
Working for a Cancer is a bit like driving along a freeway
through the Baltic states: lots of signs, no explanations, and the
ever-present chance of explosions.

To call a Cancer bastard boss "moody," however, is about as
pinpoint accurate as calling the Sultan of Brunei "well off,"
Michael Jackson "a bit odd," or Tori Spelling "fortunate." Some
people attribute Cancer's dramatic swings in temper and de-
meanor to the lunar phases. In the case of Cancer bastard
bosses, however, the cause is solar, the sun often being in a
position to cause both Irritable Bowel Syndrome and Chronic
Chili Bum.

On Monday, the chances are that the boss will stride, even skip, into the office, belly a-wobble with mirth, and keep everybody entertained for almost four hours with tales of adventure and derring-do (somebody *else*'s adventure and derring-do, of course). Your dentures will dislodge and your coffee cup go flying as the boss claps you heartily on the back and tells you that *you're making a positive contribution to the accounts*, which is Cancerspeak for *I'm not going to sack you today*.

On Tuesday, however, it's clear that there's been some sunspot activity. The boss will likely enter, thunderous looks and bulging neck veins readily visible, and bellow on about how only half the scheduled workload was completed the day before. You will be told, at deafening volume, that *greater attention has to be paid to individual efficiencies*, a phrase which, roughly translated, means *I may well sack you this afternoon if you so much as hint at taking a lunch break*.

Wednesday all will be balmy again, until you mention, innocently enough and by way of casual pleasantry, that you are rather looking forward to the hairdresser's appointment you've made for that evening. In an instant, the eyes will narrow and an Ice Age will descend. The door to the executive cubby-hole will slam shut and not another word will be heard all day.

Nor all day Thursday. Nor Friday. This is because, given the intense personal secrecy of the Cancer bastard boss, you could not, of course, have known that your employer's last, tragic and deeply painful relationship had been with a hairdresser. Reminded of this by your callous remark, the poor dear has ever since been sitting under the desk, knees at chest, silent, weep-

ing and mournful, refusing to come out even when poked at
with a cattle-prod by the secretary, or cajoled by a crack team of
police negotiators and sundry desperate relatives equipped
with loud hailers and sodden hankies.

Truly, there is never a dull moment with a Cancer bastard
boss. Lots and lots of really *horrible* ones, yes. But dull ones, no.

There is little any employee can do, in the final analysis,
about the Cancer mood swings, short of becoming addicted to
opium (a perfectly acceptable strategy, by the way, if you happen to work in the public service, where sudden movements
tend to startle). Any employee with a half-developed sense of
self-preservation, however, can at least learn how to interpret
what the old bastard says. (An employee with a *fully* developed
sense of self-preservation in a Cancer-run work place is, of
course, a contradiction in terms.)

Here, then, is a handy cut-out-and-keep guide to understanding the Cancer bastard boss.

If the Boss Says:	It Means:
You're always calm in a crisis.	You don't work hard enough.
I don't believe in judging books by their covers, do you?	Your shirt is nauseating. Wear it again at your peril.
The customer is always right.	The next time I see you trying to talk a blind, crippled pensioner out of buying one of our home gymnasiums, you're sacked.

If the Boss Says:	It Means:
It's time this company had a sexual harassment policy.	Will you come to dinner with me?
I'll be away till Tuesday at a high-level conference in Nevada.	Me and 20 other suited sleaze-bags will be having a long weekend in Las Vegas.
These are difficult days.	I'm about to sack you.
These are very difficult days.	I'm about to sack everybody.
So, is this a social call?	I sacked you last week. Didn't you notice?
Can I talk to you for a minute?	You're sacked.
Are you happy here?	You're sacked.
I was impressed by your last report.	I feel threatened. You're sacked.
It's important to keep one's emotions in check.	Stop grovelling. You're still sacked.
Be sensible and put down that gun.	Be sensible, and put down that gun.

How to Get a Raise.

Upping your wages under a Cancer bastard boss is simplicity itself. The only thing you have to bear in mind is the timing.

There is not a mood in the human repertoire which the Cancer bastard boss does not demonstrate, from simpering gratitude to furious rage. The key—and the trick—is to pick the right one. It is of critical importance that you bide your time until the boss is feeling happy, generous, optimistic and expansive.

According to our calculations, this is very likely to be on Thursday, August 14, 2007, between 3:15 P.M. and 5:45 P.M.[1]

How to Get a Promotion.

It gets lonely at the top, and Cancer bastard bosses, being very reluctant to confide in anyone, feel this loneliness more than most.

Winning a better position is therefore dependent on winning the trust of the boss. Try to convince him or her that you care, that it grieves you to see such a heavy burden resting on one pair of shoulders (no matter how broad), that you've always been of the opinion that a problem shared is a problem halved, and that, well, should the need to talk ever arise, *you'll be there.*

It's a long-shot, but you never know. You may well, a few days later, find yourself staying back and nodding intermittently as the boss's tale of woe and worry pours forth, a tangible sense of camaraderie developing between the two of you.

If this happens, you can be certain that the next senior vacancy to crop up is yours. You can also be certain that the boss was adopted as a baby, and that someone in the adoption agency at the time made a fairly significant clerical error.

Real Cancer bastard bosses would never fall for such a ploy. Real Cancer bastard bosses are assholes.

---

[1] Yes, yes, we know August 14, 2007 is a Tuesday. Thank you, Virgo.

How to Get the Bastard's Job.

This is tricky, not least because securing the boss's job presupposes that you know what it is the boss actually *does*. In a Cancer-run work environment, it's very likely that this information will be regarded as confidential.

On the other hand, if the mood is favorable, he or she may be perfectly willing to tell all, in a way which only Cancer bastard bosses truly can.

"Excuse me, but what exactly do you do?" you could ask.

"*Well,*" would come the reply, "*I facilitate the delivery of diverse services to certain demographics by the astute management of investment capital and human resources, leading to a net surplus of income over expenditure and the maintenance of the viability of the corporate entity.*"

"Maintenance!" you will then say. "I can do that. Hand me the mop and a Swiss army knife. How about a partnership, bud?"

You will then be given a short—but, as it turns out, directly applicable—lecture on the periodic need to *deploy certain astringencies in adjusting labor force capabilities.*

The unemployment office is about three blocks up the road, by the way. Turn left at the liquor store.

THE SCORPIO BASTARD BOSS

October 24–November 22

If a market researcher[2] was to round up the entire world supply of Scorpio bastard bosses, and stick the lot of them in a
very large room, there would be only three possible outcomes:

1. Within a matter of seconds, said-same Scorpios would be
standing with their backs against the walls, casting suspicious
sideways glances at each other.

2. In their absence at the offices where they usually preside,
there would be a dramatic fall in demand for essential necessi-

---

[2] If, however, the same market researcher were to round up the entire world supply
of Scorpio bastard bosses and put them in liquid cement, it would be a good start.

ties like electronic surveillance systems, concurrent with a rapid rise in orders for luxury items such as tea bags, Oreos, desks and computers.

3. All employees, after receiving their requested consignment of PCs, would be frantically searching the Internet for instructions on how to make destructive and deadly bombs.

If the same market researcher was then to gather up every person who ever entered a Scorpio-run office on a regular basis, then herded them into an adjacent, even bigger room, the outcome would be equally as predictable:

"Man, dropping off deliveries to that bastard's office gives me the fuckin' creeps."   *(MOTORCYCLE COURIER)*

"Yes, all the staff there seem alarmingly twitchy."

(DOOR-TO-DOOR SALESMAN SELLING FOR

MOTOR NEURONE DISABILITY CHARITY)

"I'm not thurprithed, thweetie. When even I grayth the playth with my prethenth, ith ath if there'th alwayth thomeone thpying on me to thee if I'm thkimping on the flowerth."

(FLOWER DELIVERY MAN)

"Well, I really resent the way His Nibs insists upon counting every single piece of paper in a 500-sheet ream before signing the goddamned order."   *(STATIONERY SUPPLIER)*

"Would any of you like to buy a copy of *Watch Tower*?"

(JEHOVAH'S WITNESS)

"No, get lost. I'm going into the next room to plant this deadly and destructive bomb. I expect I'll water it, too."   *(You)*

Of course, at this point, what you and your fellow conspirators fail to realize is that the Scorpio bastards next door have been listening to your exchange through the walls and are now placing cryptic mobile phone calls to their underworld contacts.

To any Scorpio in a position of power, *forewarned is forearmed.* To you and every other poor sod who has to work for one, *eavesdroppers hear no good of themselves, particularly if they happen to be Scorpio bastard bosses.*

Because they've positioned time clocks at exit and entrance points, as well as padlocked the petty cash tin, the bar fridge and the stationery cupboard, Scorpio employers always jump to the conclusion that one employee or another will thus be hatching plots to rip them off or knock them off.

However, they can't just act on such suspicions willy-nilly. Concrete evidence is needed. Therefore, those Scorpio employers in charge of large budgets like to verify such wild accusations by installing closed-circuit cameras in offices and lavatories alike. To gather more unassailable proof of treachery and treason in the ranks, they'll also plant bugs underneath desks and inside telephone handpieces.

Such vigilance on their part might be understandable if, say, they were heading up a foreign intelligence unit, the Cosa Nostra, or a political party. It does seem somewhat of a rather unnecessary evil in, say, an apple orchard.

Unfortunately, even if a sudden down-turn in business neces-
sitated drastic cost-cutting measures that included the slashing
of expenditure on electronic spying devices (and only after friv-
olous fancies like pens, paper and flowers for the foyer have
gotten the chop first), Scorpio employers are perfectly well-
equipped with their own internal antennae.

As sure as Scorpio bosses are stealthy, sneaky bastards, the
minute you contemplate placing a social call, a dark shadow will
loom over your speed dial. The second you even consider reading a cheap and trashy magazine instead of writing a report,
something cold and icy will start breathing down your neck.
And the moment you so much as think of leaving the office
early, something akin to the creature from a black lagoon will
emerge from behind.

It would not be too gross an exaggeration to say that most
employees working for a Scorpio bastard boss spend so much
time looking over their shoulders, they keep bumping into
walls and falling down elevator shafts. Moreover, when they do
cast those long and lingering backward glances, what they witness is a pretty horrible sight.

It's not the dark cape, the scythe, nor the terrifying eyes
burning in the death-mask skull that disturb most. No, it's the
white rubber-soled sports shoes that the boss insists upon
wearing with the three-piece corporate suit. They're enough
to give any discerning employee the screaming ab-dabs. And
they do, frequently. The eerie silence that invariably envelops
a Scorpio-run office is only ever broken by high-pitched yelps
from those workers unfortunate enough to have been sprung

just as they were about to laugh at their employer's peculiar dress sense.

Sinister and creepy as they are, occasionally Scorpio bosses will be forced to smile—usually when they think they've caught you red-handed. Doing what, you have no idea, since they won't actually tell you. Scorpios aren't big on small talk. They prefer to let you prattle on, protesting your innocence, while they remain deep in thought, invariably thinking up suitably nasty punishments for your purported crimes.

In the dark netherworld that is the Scorpio mind, all employees are guilty until proven so.

In fact, being called to question by a Scorpio boss is rather like being pulled over by the police when your car is fully registered, you haven't been speeding or run a red light, and your last drink was imbibed three years ago. *You will still feel guilty about the fact that you haven't got your grandmother's corpse stashed under the picnic rug in the trunk.*

One look from that frightening, penetrating gaze and you'll be confessing to all kinds of crimes, none of which are in the least bit true. Well, most of them, anyway. You lied about your grandmother. She's not dead. She's resting.

Don't think you can escape the terrifying retribution that is sure to follow. Playing on your employer's sympathies simply won't work. Excessive displays of emotion are not to be tolerated in a Scorpio workplace. Blubbing, wailing, sobbing, snifling, weeping and bleating, in particular, are strictly off limits. Needless to say, this has always struck you as strange, given that the bastard manages to reduce you to tears within a matter of seconds after wrongly accusing you of playing on his or her sympathies.

Buttering up the boss will get you nowhere, either. Why are you being so nice? What's your hidden motive? Nothing, you truthfully reply, given that the letter opener—the one with the ten inch blade that can kill a Scorpio bastard boss in less time than it takes to slice, dice and chop a carrot—is lying frustratingly out of arm's reach in your own office.

But, really, so what if your boss is an uptight, suspicious and utterly paranoid sociopath? It's hardly going to kill you, is it?

Er, well, actually, yes it is.

If you ever thought your life wasn't worth living while working for a Scorpio, your employer will confirm it if you attempt to leave.

Scorpios demand the same kind of loyalty from their charges that certain hoodlums of Mediterranean stock always inspire. Many an employee has been shocked to receive a pair of concrete shoes instead of a gold watch upon retirement. Many more are distressed when, having sensibly fled before the age of 55, they find themselves being shadowed to their new place of work by cauliflower-eared henchmen, toting machine guns disguised as violin cases.

Thus, under threat of death and fear of reprisal, those employees toiling under the black-hooded, black-clouded reign of a Scorpio bastard boss are remarkably quiet, subdued and extremely work-efficient. The receptionist wouldn't dream of keeping clients on hold so she can take a social call. The accountant would never cook the books, let alone cut the espionage expense account. The flower delivery man doesn't ever try skimping on the flowers. And you wouldn't be seen dead reading *The National Enquirer* during office hours. No way. You're far too busy plotting your Scorpio chief's comeuppance.

Just to prove the bastard right for a change.

How to Get a Raise.

This is the fiscal equivalent of getting blood out of a stone, photocopier toner out of a white shirt and a Taurean's head out of a cookie jar. Even if you do manage to squeeze more money from your Scorpio bastard boss—a feat only likely to be achieved by introducing medieval instruments of torture—then expect to pay for it dearly for the rest of your working life.

In fact, why not prepare early? Buy a dictaphone (or steal the one your boss uses to tape meetings, interviews and employees) and enlist a colleague with a suitably deep and quietly ominous voice to say something along the lines of: "You *do* realize that I can neither forget nor forgive you for this?" to the sound of thumbscrews being tightened and a rack being stretched. Play the tape at regular intervals throughout the day. Then decide if a five percent pay rise is really worth the bother.

How to Get a Promotion.

Unswerving loyalty tends to pay dividends in a Scorpio-run office. Unfortunately, *unswerving loyalty* translates as *working with the company until the day you die without being caught pilfering so much as a paper clip.* Then, and only then, will you be considered worthy of promotion. If time is not on your side, and honesty is not one of your strong points, you may have to resort to more drastic measures in order to get a leg up the corporate ladder.

May we suggest loitering in the staff bathrooms, with letter-opener at the ready? When the boss eventually shows up to replace the battery in the security camera above the wash basins, creep up from behind, press cold blade against executive jugular and threaten to steal the bastard's Nike Air runners if you don't get a better job position within the next 24 hours.

How to Get the Bastard's Job.

Don't even try following in your Scorpio employer's footsteps. Otherwise, you'll end up taking over the latter's cowed and resentful workers, accompanied by the predictable death threats, bomb scares and assassination attempts. Even on the dole, the bastard never gives up.

THE PISCES BASTARD BOSS

February 20–March 20

While there are, no doubt, plenty of Pisceans collecting shopping trolleys in car parks, or rooting through landfills in search of things to sell at the markets, or picking up leaves with those long stick things on driveways of apartment blocks during blustery autumn months, there will be few, if any, fellow fish barking swift and efficient orders from the sidelines.[3]

This is because *there is no such thing as a Piscean bastard boss.* Trainees, apprentices, cadets, juniors and bottle washers, yes. Chiefs, leaders, governors, directors and presidents, no.

---

[3]Yes, yes, Virgo, we realize that fish don't actually bark *per se*. It's called a *metaphor*. Now, *do* shut up . . .

Other astrologers will dispute this, of course, usually because they feel sorry for the poor bastards. However, cold, hard scientific, medical and historical facts confirm:

a) Nine out of ten cats prefer their fish served up to them alive and in one piece. Nine out of ten employees who have ever worked for a fish of the Piscean variety disagree.

b) Eighty percent of midwives concede that babies delivered between February 20 and March 20 in any given year are usually missing the full set of vertebrae and brain cells needed to provide the constitution and mind-set to take on major responsibility of any kind.

c) Historians unanimously agree that, through time immemorial, those few Pisceans who foolishly thought they had leadership potential were ruthlessly weeded out at lower management level by discerning corporate recruitment agencies who valued their reputation as discerning corporate recruitment agencies.

Working on these premises, and wishing to keep our professional integrity intact, we'd resolved to ditch this chapter completely. However, faced with eight or so blank pages in the middle of a volume of work that could at best be described slim, our publisher threw an impressive hissy fit (he's a fire sign), demanded to know what was wrong with saying things we didn't mean in order to keep someone happy (he's a Leo), and told us that if we really valued our jobs we'd do it pronto (he's a bastard boss).

So, for the sake of some peace and quiet, and under threat of losing a rather hefty advance, we're going to ask you to pretend, if you will, that your bastard boss also happens to be a Piscean.

Er, okay. Now what?

Well, while you're sitting in the boardroom at ten past two in the afternoon waiting for your hypothetical boss to turn up to the 11 A.M. meeting, you could start making a list of all the reasons why Pisceans never get ahead in advertising, or any other trade for that matter:

1. Irresponsible

You could then deliberate as to why, when your erstwhile employer eventually does show up at five in the evening, he or she blames such tardiness on the alarm clock, the spouse, the drug habit and/or the Communists:

1. Irresponsible
2. Irresponsible

You might also like to question as to why, during the meeting, your boss starts serving up finger food and beverages to the clients when there's a perfectly proficient member of the catering staff being paid by the hour, standing by:

1. Irresponsible
2. Irresponsible
3. Great big suck-up

Finally, when the meeting's over, and your boss proceeds to while away the hours mopping down the boardroom table and stacking the dishwasher in a decidedly slapdash, slipshod manner, knowing full well there's a mountain of more important, pressing work to be done in an equally slapdash, slipshod manner, you could add:

1. Irresponsible
2. Irresponsible
3. Great big suck-up
4. Irresponsible

By now you would have reached the not-so-startling conclusion that Piscean employers would be enormously dangerous in positions of power. Mostly because they would be irresponsible and great big suck-ups.

Pisces bastard bosses wouldn't know what to do with power even if someone was stupid enough to give them some. In fact, how they would have managed to get the number one job in the first place would be beyond their own (let alone *your*) realms of comprehension. However, for argument's sake, in the current scenario, let's pretend that the international CEO had no choice but to appoint a Pisces to head the company you work for, because the 550 more suitable candidates were killed in a debilitating home hygiene mishap.

Piscean employers—if there were such a thing—would act exactly like *employees*. That is, not only would they shirk work, steal from the stationery cupboard, and try to sleep with that new girl from dispatch at the annual Christmas party, they'd also park themselves on a seat next to you in the staff canteen every day and beg you to share their sandwiches. The more naive employee (that is, *you*) would mistake this for a solidarity of sorts and happily swap your smoked salmon on rye for some sub-standard peanut butter and jelly soldiers. Of course, what Piscean bosses would really be trying to do is blend in with the rest of the staff so that no one can specifically point the finger at them when they screw up.

In the tough, unforgiving world of business, the buck stops at the boss. But not with a Piscean it wouldn't. Said buck would be caught with about as much enthusiasm as a sexually trans-mitted virus, then lobbed swiftly and deftly back onto someone else's shoulders. A Pisces boss would call this *delegation*. You'd probably call it *abnegation of responsibility* though, hell, what would you know? You finished school, attended university and graduated *cum laude*, which is more than you would be able to say for that cowering little creep who's meant to be sitting in the corner office.

Because they're such sensitive souls, and don't like being yelled at by you or anyone else, Pisces bastard bosses would always try one of two escape plans. The first would be to blame someone else. And they would do it so soulfully, and with so much hand wringing, and piteous sniffling, that you'd most likely feel a burning rage at Julie from the mail room for being directly responsible for the dramatic collapse of the entire com-pany. If, however, you didn't swallow that, Piscean bosses would opt for Plan B. This would entail either standing on the ledge of the twelfth floor office window and threatening to electrocute themselves, or sitting in the midst of the typing pool threatening to hang themselves with a staple gun.

Your outpouring of sympathy would usually come to an abrupt halt sooner or later—usually when it was your turn to cop the blame. When the international CEO flies over on a rescue mission and races into the staff canteen saying "Who's the fucking idiot in charge of this mess?," your Pisces bastard boss would squeak "Not me!," and point at whichever muggins was standing closest by. You, in turn, maw agape, would end up trotting behind your superior's superior to do some serious scapegoating.

In some kinder, less vicious astrological circles, it is deemed that Pisceans are leading lights in certain fields. Like the arts, for instance. Look at Michelangelo. A Piscean master who managed to capture the imagination of many a budding artist.

Yes. One can only imagine the sight of his protégés standing under the Sistine Chapel ceiling, craning their necks, feeling the relentless drip of paint plopping onto their eyeballs as they reverentially chirrup: "Er, nice work, Mick. But how about painting it on the wall next time so you can see it without getting bloody whiplash?"

The same do-gooder shamans of the stars even go so far as declaring Pisceans geniuses, often putting forward one Albert Einstein as proof thereof. While we wouldn't dream of questioning this eminent physicist's intellectual capacities, we suspect he might have been born on a cusp.

✳ ✳ ✳

And finally, celestial ambulance-chasers will vehemently deny charges that all Pisces bastard bosses are self-serving cowards who wouldn't risk their own neck to save an employee, even if the latter was drowning. We have only five words to say to that: *Ted Kennedy is a Pisces.*

Pisces bastard bosses, if they existed, would definitely be good for nothing. However, since we haven't quite run out of writing space yet, we'll continue to be responsible for the senseless demise of yet another innocent rain forest by making up some things that Piscean employers can do without any supervision from you:

✳ Staring out of windows during boardroom meetings.

✳ Agreeing with everything everyone says.

✳ Making coffee (so long as it's instant and doesn't have to be percolated, filtered, plunged or poured).

✳ Developing drug habits in order to expedite elaborate suicide attempts.

✳ Staging elaborate suicide attempts to get attention/ sympathy/let off the hook.

✳ Picking up leaves outside the office foyer using one of those long stick things.

How to Get a Raise.

All Pisces bastard bosses would immediately agree to your out-
landish proposal for tripling your salary overnight—mainly
because you would have wisely proposed it on a Friday and
they wouldn't want to be bitched about later over office
drinks, especially since they've volunteered to serve behind
the bar again. Should your request be rejected by some curmudgeonly killjoy in the accounting department come Monday morning, it wouldn't be their fault, despite the fact they
would be the ones in charge of overriding said curmudgeonly
killjoy.

How to Get a Promotion.

Easy. As soon as your Pisces bastard boss realizes he or she
might be held accountable for making a balls-up of an entire
organization, all of a sudden you would be in charge of 300
employees, five offices nationwide, 12 factory outlets and an
overseas subsidiary. This would come as a bit of a shock to you if
you were previously the cleaner.

How to Get the Bastard's Job.

Let's put it this way. You've got more chance of getting it than a Pisces employer ever has. And that's all we've got to say on the matter because our Leo bastard boss is in the background, frantically signaling that any more words and the paper stock budget is going to blow out.

GETTING THE BETTER OF
BASTARD
BOSSES

Unfortunately for the legions of us condemned to a life of wage slavery, long hours, low pay, and crappy instant coffee in the staff canteen, the 12 bastard bosses of the zodiac are violent, stubborn, lazy, moody, vain, picky, indecisive, mean, annoying, snobbish, sanctimonious, ineffective, and, worst of all, *nearby*.

Whatever their faults, however, it is important to remember that they are all also *human*. Well, human*oid*. Okay, *ape-like*, then. All right, can we agree on *multi-cellular*?

And therein lies their greatest weakness, a weakness which *you*, a loyal employee with a proud astrological heritage of your own, can ruthlessly manipulate for your personal gain. Let's face it, their faults are not exactly difficult to spot—easier to pick, even, than a dog turd smeared across the Mona Lisa.

If there is one thing the caring and sharing nineties have taught us it is this: if someone has a problem, it is your *duty* to get in there, as fast as possible, and exploit the hell out of it for everything you can. And if that someone happens to be a bastard boss, then so much the better. You don't even have to feel guilty afterward.

This is not a world of equality. The bastard bosses will always have larger salaries, greater power, bigger houses, faster cars, better clothes and fatter stomachs than you. They will always have more of *everything* than you, including—and this is the important bit—more to *lose*.

Which is where you come in.

As an employee, you have a sworn responsibility to your fellow workers to put one over on the boss every chance you get. Stand up for yourself! Organize! Fight for better pay and conditions! Strike! Picket! Demand justice! Demand—

Pardon? Yes, Your Magnificence. Sorry. We'll be quiet now, and finish licking clean your Jaguar, shall we, just like you told us to . . .

THE ARIES SLAVE

March 21–April 20

While some of your more timid peers may caution you to tread warily through working life, at least you can hold your own in front of the panel of 12 bastard bosses seated before you. Because, as a straight-shooting tough-talking Aries, you make no apologies for who you are and what you want from day one (which just happens to be the job interview).

ARIES BASTARD BOSS: Do you take orders?
YOU: No.
ARIES BASTARD BOSS: List your faults then.

YOU: No.

ARIES BASTARD BOSS *(shouting)*: I said: LIST! YOUR! FAULTS!.

YOU *(suddenly realizing it's you who wants the job)*: I have none . . . but I can make some up if it would make you feel better about yourself.

ARIES BASTARD BOSS: Don't have time . . . Where do you see yourself in five years from now?

YOU *(curling lip)*: Hopefully visiting *you* in a retirement village.

CAPRICORN BASTARD BOSS: Speaking of pension funds, how much are you being paid currently?

YOU: Well, considering that jacket you're wearing, probably a hell of a lot more than you.

CAPRICORN BASTARD BOSS *(whipping out calculator)*: What are your assets then?

YOU *(completely missing the point)*: I'm intelligent, hardworking, personable, a born salesman, a natural leader . . .

TAURUS BASTARD BOSS *(apropos of nothing)*: Are you argumentative?

YOU *(too quickly)*: No.

TAURUS BASTARD BOSS: Are too!

YOU: Am not!

TAURUS BASTARD BOSS: Are too!

YOU: Am not!

PISCES BASTARD BOSS *(piteously)*: Please, let's not fight.

YOU *(belligerently)*: Why not?

PISCES BASTARD BOSS: Because you'll upset my delicate equilibrium.

YOU: Ha, ha, ha. Tee-hee-hee. Haw, haw, haw. Heh, heh, heh.

GEMINI BASTARD BOSS *(laughing with you because he hasn't been paying attention)*: Are you flexible?

YOU: You mean, will I bend over backward for you?

GEMINI BASTARD BOSS: I mean, are you willing to work a few extra hours, here and there, if need be?

YOU: You mean, do all your work as well?

GEMINI BASTARD BOSS: Yes.

EMBARRASSED SILENCE FROM EVERYONE ELSE.

AQUARIUS BASTARD BOSS *(apropos of nothing)*: So, what do you think about the wanton rape of the rain forests?

YOU *(completely flummoxed)*: What?

AQUARIUS BASTARD BOSS: What do you think about the unmitigated capitalistic exploitation of the global community's natural heritage?

YOU: Well, I've never tried it, but I'd be willing to give it a go.

AWKWARD PAUSE.

SCORPIO BASTARD BOSS *(suspiciously)*: Why did you leave your last job?

YOU: Because I worked for a bastard Scorpio who sexually harassed me.

SCORPIO BASTARD BOSS: Are you sure you weren't deliberately leading him on?

YOU: Well, I suppose given that I'm a drop-dead gorgeous 20-year-old blond bombshell with big tits who didn't want anything to do with a fat old creep with bad teeth, you could have a point there.

LIBRA BASTARD BOSS *(hurriedly interrupting in order to avoid a scene)*: Um, er, do you find decision-making easy?

YOU *(hackles rising)*: I find that a very insulting and demeaning question coming from *you*.

LIBRA BASTARD BOSS: Look, no offense . . . er, what do you think, Leo?

LEO BASTARD BOSS: Do you like my new haircut?

YOU *(reluctantly)*: It's all *right* . . .

LEO BASTARD BOSS: You think so? You're not just saying that because you want the job?

YOU: Yes.

LEO BASTARD BOSS *(confident you must be just joking)*: Very funny. So why do you want this job?

YOU: In order to really piss you off by stealing *your* thunder for a change and reducing you to a mass of insecurities, thereby making you a lot more endearing to all and sundry.

CANCER BASTARD BOSS *(attempting the lowest form of wit)*: You're obviously very sensitive to other people's feelings?

YOU: Of course I am, you bonehead.

CANCER BASTARD BOSS: There's no need to get nasty.

YOU *(confused)*: But I haven't even started yet.

VIRGO BASTARD BOSS *(determined to get his questions in)*: What do you think you can bring to this company?

YOU: More than you ever have *(realizing slip and back-pedalling furiously)*, and I mean that in the most respectful way, of course.

VIRGO BASTARD BOSS *(not noticing veiled insult as too busy referring to a manual entitled* "Successful Interviewing Techniques"*)*: Who is your role model?

YOU *(playing for obligatory laugh as instructed by* "How to Win Over an Interviewer"*)*: Pisces.

SNIGGERS ALL ROUND.

SAGITTARIUS BASTARD BOSS *(borrowing Virgo's book from him)*: Are you a team player?

YOU: As long as I'm in charge, yes.

SAGITTARIUS BASTARD BOSS: Do you like a challenge?

YOU: If it means working with you, no.

Interview now over, the 12 bastards shuffle off to the anteroom to discuss your prospects while you make yourself at home at the head of the boardroom table. Aries, Taurus and Sagittarius believe you're too big for your boots. Libra and Gemini reckon you're a real wag. Cancer thinks you're about as funny as him. Aquarius and Virgo don't quite understand you. Leo feels threatened. And Pisces thinks you're mean. But, leader of the pack, Scorpio, thinks you've got nice legs and a really cute bum. You're hired.

THE TAURUS SLAVE

April 21–May 21

This is going to be tricky, you think, given that your qualifications and experience, on paper at least, look a little, well, *thin*. Never mind. You are Taurean. And you want this job. That's all that matters.

"So," asks the **Virgo Bastard Boss** (Editor: Business, Stock Market), "what makes you think you can be the New York correspondent for this newspaper?"

You consider your answer at length. It *has* to be a trick question. Then again, maybe not. "Bio-chemical activity in the front part of my brain," you reply.

"Needs a well-traveled man, the New York desk," pants the

Sagittarius Bastard Boss (Travel, Sport). "Where did you go on your last holidays?"

You are prepared for this one. "I do not believe in mixing business and pleasure," you say, "so I stayed at home."

"Do you have any contacts in New York?" asks the **Capricorn Bastard Boss** (Social Pages, Obituaries, Weather).

"Could you clarify the word 'contacts'?" you reply.

"Do you *know* anybody there?"

"Let's see," you muse. "Seventeen million people in the city, so, yes, I'd say there was a pretty good chance I'll find a familiar face. Robert De Niro, for instance."

"You *know* Robert De Niro?" gasps the **Leo Bastard Boss** (Entertainment, Columns, Those Self-Important Pompous Rambles You Find In The Sunday Editions).

"No," you reply, "but I'm sure I'd recognize him. He's on television sometimes, isn't he?"

"I was on television once," mumbles the **Cancer Bastard Boss** (Women's Pages, Poetry). This is good, you think. The chance for major brownie points.

"*That's* where I've seen you before," you smile. "What was it? Don't tell me. Yes. *America's Most Wanted.*"

You notice that the Cancer Bastard has now pulled his jacket over his head and is noisily sucking his thumb. Not so good, maybe, you think.

"Should you get this position," rumbles the **Scorpio Bastard Boss** (Politics, Police, Organized Crime), "you may well have to interview the president. How would you go about that?"

You are confident here. You have done your research. "I

would approach that in two phases," you say. "First, I would ask him questions. Second, I would write down his answers."

"The second part sounds novel, but it just might work," nods the **Gemini Bastard Boss** (Whatever No One Else Wants To Do). "You might also have to visit the United Nations and talk to distinguished foreign ambassadors. Do you think you're fully prepared for that?"

You have to be careful here. You've researched as much as you could, but you fell asleep before you reached "U" in the guide book. Up as far as Trump Tower, you're fine; after that, mystery. "Prepared in exactly what sense?" you ask.

The Gemini Bastard looks suddenly taken aback. He blinks rapidly and stares around the room for a clue. "Ah, exactly what sense would you prefer?" he stammers.

"He *means*," interrupts the **Libra Bastard Boss** (Fashion, Homeware, Fabric News, Fawning Profiles Of Naomi Campbell), sighing as if dealing with a particularly stupid child, "do you own a *suit?*"

Ahh. "Oh, yes," you reply. "Two. Both Armani."

"Difficult job, the New York post," snaps the **Aries Bastard Boss** (Foreign News, Industrial Relations, Pictures Of Masked Men With Machetes). "Lot of work. Then there's the time difference. When it's midday here, it's midnight there. What makes you think you could do the job better than I could?"

You've read about this. It's called "flattery." You hope you can remember how to do it. "I'm sure I couldn't," you smile. "But I'm prepared to work at it day and night. Simultaneously."

An unimpressed grunting noise comes from the other side of the room. It's the **Taurus Bastard Boss** (Books, Crosswords, Interminably Long And Turgid Leading Articles). "Do you intend to make a habit of flattering your editors?" he asks.

"I don't know yet," you reply. "I'll wait to see if it works."

"And what," asks the **Pisces Bastard Boss** (Stars, Children's Pages, Conspiracy Theories), "did you do on your last newspaper?"

"Wrote a telephone number in the margin of the back page, that's all," you say, and then realize what he meant. "Ahh, yes. The same as I've been doing on this one."

The Pisces editor has somehow managed to get his shoe stuck in the wastepaper basket. Trying to get it out, he asks, "And that is?"

This, you reflect, could be the tricky bit. "Oh, lots of stuff: stand at the front door in a blue uniform, hand out visitors' passes, take packages from couriers. Whatever needs doing, really."

"Let me get this straight," says the **Aquarius Bastard Boss** (Lifestyles, Social Justice, Photographs Of Baby Fur Seals). "You're saying you are not, in fact, a highly trained senior journalist with a minimum of five years in an overseas posting, as per the advert, but, in fact, one of the security guards downstairs who are always telling me I can't bring my bicycle into the office."

You were right. This *is* the tricky bit. "Well," you say, "you have to have *rules*, don't you?"

"But *what*," continues Aquarius, "makes you think that qualifies you to become our New York correspondent?"

"Well," you say, "I can handle a gun. And I've got security camera video which shows four of you drinking on the job, six of you smoking in the toilets, and two of you having sex on the managing director's desk."

There follows a moment of silence. "Okay. Thank you," says the Libra Bastard Boss. "Would you be free to fly out on Friday?"

THE GEMINI SLAVE

May 22–June 21

It's Monday, 9 A.M. Having showered, dressed and shaved in record time, you're charging out your front door when, all of a sudden, you realize you've forgotten something. Your job. You don't have one anymore. You got removed from the cookie factory conveyor line yesterday because, in an attempt to keep yourself amused for longer than a split-second, you got caught trying to devise a new biscuit hybrid by cloning a Ginger Snap with a Mallomar (ending up with a soft thing full of crunchy bits which slashed half your tongue off).

So, it's back indoors again and time to do unemployed kind of things—so you smoke a bong, try out your Thighmaster, call a friend, write a letter, prepare then eat a Hot Pocket, and watch a couple of soaps.

It is now 9:03 A.M. You have been officially unemployed for three minutes and you are bored beyond belief. Desperate for distraction, you decide to pick up the newspaper and scan the classifieds for another job.

> **Aries Bastard Boss** demands disciplined, hard-working perfectionist with ability to take orders and participate in rallies, parades and unarmed combat. Mustn't mind working weekends. No welfare moms.

Whoa! Intense or what? This guy should lighten up. And anyway, you were briefly in the defense services before. Needless to say, it was an unmitigated disaster, particularly when, just for a laugh, you rolled the tank during field training.

> Traditional, established company, run by **Taurus Bastard Boss** requires loyal, dependable person to sell cure-alls door to door. Own horse and cart essential.

Now this one sounds really interesting. Too bad you just recently exchanged your horse for a Gameboy because it's cheaper to feed, easier to maintain, and a lot more fun to play with.

> Want to earn extra money in your own spare time?
> Then a **Gemini Bastard Boss** needs you.

Uh-oh. You've fallen for that line before. It's bad enough having to work during *working hours* for a Gemini bastard boss. And anyway, you get enough accusations of being plastic and shallow as it is, without flogging Tupperware lunch boxes for a living.

> **Cancer Bastard Boss** ooble glus coolds theisod thenslf theodkw aodkth dokw dodhwkd aoieee diopeas kipper, sob, sob, sniff, sniff.

Que? What the hell is this all about? Maybe you'd better read it again. On second thought, maybe you'd better not. Last time you attempted to understand a Cancer bastard boss your brain imploded with all that concentration.

> **Leo Bastard Boss** urgently requires ex-cult members to join quasi-religious organization run by very charismatic leader.

Nah. Sorry. Being told what to think 24 hours a day, seven days a week never really does it for you—especially since you keep forgetting exactly what it was you are meant to be thinking.

> **Virgo Bastard Boss** requires diligent, conscientious individual with a keen eye for detail to check census forms, count ballot slips, spellcheck the dictionaries, proofread telephone directories, and then photocopy all of the above. *Geminis need not apply.*

Good. That settles that one then.

> **Libra Bastard Boss** seeks strongly motivated individual to salvage what's left of 200-year-old family company. Send application to inhouse insolvency division.

Well, you're great in emergencies and positively brilliant at putting out fires. Like the one you had to put out for your last Libran boss when the idiot made a half-assed attempt to torch his company's headquarters in order to get insurance to pay for his overdue layaway account at Armani.

> **Scorpio Bastard Boss** seeks young, leggy blonde with blue eyes. P.O. Box 666.

Hmmm. Reception work. Well, looking on the positive side, it's a way of meeting new people and talking on the phone to your friends for hours. But you've worked for a Scorpio in the past. And still got the therapy bills to prove it.

> **Sagittarius Bastard Boss** searching for fit person with clean bill of health to engage in exciting job with lots of travel.

Oh why, oh why, oh why do you get the sneaking suspicion that this was the same bastard you worked for last year—the one who sent you and your colleagues on a motivationally bonding hike through 1000km of desert equipped with nothing but a can-opener and corkscrew?

> **Capricorn Bastard Boss** seeks well-connected employee with view to marriage. Listing in *Debretts*, *Fortune 500* and *Who's Who* preferred. Titles an advantage. Please enclose family crest.

No way. You'd rather go poor than work for the Royal Family.

> **Aquarius Bastard Boss** requires non-gender specific personnel for non-sexist, non-racist, non-ageist work at Asian Bride Mail Order service.

Hmm. You're all for encouraging racial harmony and spiritual growth by helping fat, old Western sleazebags find a better life and true happiness with impoverished, down-trodden Third World women—but how the hell are you supposed to fit the poor things into the mail boxes?

> **Pisces Bastard Boss** looking for people who'd like to run their own business from home and make a squillion!!! To find out more, send check for $500 to: Security Box 101, Cayman Isles, The Caribbean.

Ha! Spot the outrageous error. You're almost tempted to put a call through to the Better Business Bureau for such blatantly false and misleading advertising. Even *you* know there's no such thing as a Pisces bastard boss.

Well, that was a bit of a malarky, wasn't it? *And* you've just managed to kill another two-and-a-half minutes—maybe being one of the long-term unemployed isn't so bad after all.

THE CANCER SLAVE

June 22–July 23

Dear Mom,

9 A.M.

Great news! I'm writing you this letter while seated at my new desk! I've got a window view, *a* raise, *and a* new *job title! The plan worked! I don't think I've* ever *been so happy in my life! A view, wow! I can see cars and buses and pedestrians and, oh dear, there's a man on the pavement* kicking his dog *and . . .*

Excuse me. I can't bear it.

11 A.M.

Sorry about that. I'm better now. Anyway, it was the **Aries Bastard Boss** *who first noticed I was unhappy. It might have been because of the*

placard I was carrying, the one which said in big letters: I AM DESPER-
ATELY UNHAPPY—ASK ME WHY.

He didn't. He just told me I was being selfish. "That's all you think
about, you clerks," *he said,* "Me, me, me. Did you ever stop to think how
I *feel?*"

"I don't want to be a clerk," *I told him.* "I want to be a file allocation and form-completion operative." *Then I wept. A lot.*

Which cheered me up a bit.

He must have told **Taurus Bastard Boss,** *because the old duffer
came by and told me they didn't have file allocation and form-completion
operatives in* his *day. Apparently they had to make do with horses and
carts. I cried again, then, because you know how any mention of the word
"day" reminds me of that terrible vacation I spent with Michael in
Canada . . .*

Excuse me.

Noon

Back again. Better now. Anyway, **Gemini Bastard Boss** *came by
next. He asked me what was wrong. Of course, I said "nothing." He
said, "Oh, that's all right then." I can tell you, Mom, I bawled my eyes
out at that one. He asked what the matter was now, so I told him that
no one ever believed anything I said.* "I don't believe that," *he replied.*

By the time **Cancer Bastard Boss** *came by, I was sitting under the
desk, snuffling quietly. This didn't seem to surprise him, but he did at
least have the grace to ask what was bothering me.* "It's this desk," *I
mumbled. That did it. He burst into gales of tears. Apparently his ex-
wife had liked desks. Before I knew it, we were both underneath it. His
knees were wedged up against my nose, and my left foot was poking*

into his armpit. When he dried his eyes, about 45 minutes later, he asked me what, exactly, was wrong with my desk. "It's not big enough," I wailed. He seemed to agree with me.

Leo Bastard Boss *walked past and asked us if we were staging a re-enactment of the Trojan Wars, pretending to be in a wooden horse, and, if so, would we mind terribly if he played the part of Helen of Troy. That reminded me: Michael's middle name is Troy . . .*

Oh no, not again . . .

3 P.M.

Must remember to buy some more tissues. Anyway, then **Virgo Bastard Boss** *arrived. He told me there was no such thing as a* bigger *desk, because he had rationalized desk allocation and usage, as per the statistical data he had collected. Didn't I remember, he asked, that I'd typed up the report for him?*

I hadn't "typed up the report," I sobbed. I'd facilitated data input and storage—*why couldn't anybody* see *that?*

Omigod. Down there. Standing on the pavement. It looks like Michael. It can't be.

Libra Bastard Boss *sashayed up and suggested a compromise. If not a* bigger *desk, he said, how about a* nicer *desk. A blue one, for instance.*

It is. It is Michael.

7 P.M.

I'm working late, Mom. It's the only way I'll get this letter finished. I hope they appreciate me.

Scorpio Bastard Boss *then turned up, to collect the interest on the $50 he lent me last week. I told him I didn't have it, I couldn't afford it, not at 20 percent compound per day, not on* my *wages. He told me, very* slowly and quietly, that I'd better find the funds, or I'd end up going on a long holiday.

Which, of course, reminded me of Michael again and that dreadful incident in Vancouver. I didn't cry, though. A stony silence was the best I could manage. He's still down there. Michael. Looking up at me. He's holding a bunch of red roses. It's almost enough to make me upgrade my mood from miserable to morose.

9 P.M.

It was three days before I spoke again, and only then because if **Sagittarius Bastard Boss** had asked me one more time whether a good jog around the park would cheer me up I was going to kick him in the executive nuts.

Michael, Mom, is now standing on the pavement and waving a sign up at my window. It says: I LOVE YOU. PLEASE FORGIVE ME. I think I'll try wistful melancholia for a while.

Capricorn Bastard Boss got involved next. She sidled up, patted my shoulder, sat me down and made me a cup of tea. She said she knew how I felt. A friend of hers had been through just the same sort of experience. She asked me if I knew her friend. Arch someone. Hang on. Arch Bishop. I said, no, I didn't.

"Then what the hell am I talking to you for, you pathetic little nonentity?" she spat, and walked off. That set me off again, I can tell you.

Oh, look: Michael is blowing me kisses. I shall pretend to ignore him.

10 P.M.

Aquarius Bastard Boss called an emergency meeting—a workshop, he called it—to discuss the situation. He said that, clearly, giving me a wage raise would help, and that the spare desk by the window would be better in terms of the building's feng shui, *whatever that is. He also offered to give me some acupuncture. Said it would make me feel better.*

I agreed, but as he inserted the first needle I felt a little prick, which, of course, made me think about Michael again. (A hint, Mom: never sob convulsively with a two-inch piece of surgical steel stuck in your abdomen.*)*

It's raining outside. That'll teach Michael to chat up Canadian barmaids when he's out with me.

Finally, **Pisces Bastard Boss** *said none of this was* his *fault (it never is), but I could have my new job title if it meant they could all get a bit of peace and quiet. He even said he'd do the engraving for my desk sign himself. He did. I am now, officially, a* Feel Application And Firm Complexion Operator. *I'll get used to it, I'm sure.*

Oh dear. Michael is now running across the wet road toward the building. Could it be because I just held a sign up in the window, saying: COME TO MY ARMS, ALL IS FORGIVEN? *Surely not. Tut tut. Look at that. Right in front of a bus. Thump. Splat. Ah well. All's well that ends well. I feel so happy I could cry.*

Yours forever,

Cancer.

THE LEO SLAVE

July 24–August 23

No Leo, yourself included, was put in this world to serve other people. Your superhuman talents and supernatural good looks equip you for nothing less than master or mistress of the entire universe. However, if you still haven't yet made it from hall monitor to CEO in one effortless leap, it's obviously because your current employers have refused to give you the glowing praise you deserve on the grounds that, like the mere earthlings they are, they're stupid, ignorant and can't be trusted to do anything by themselves. With this in mind, you're just going to have to write your own references.

TO WHOM IT MAY CONCERN

Company lawyers have advised me not to comment upon the performance of this particular employee. However, since I'm the one in charge round here, not them, I will say that Leo is overreacting somewhat to our trifling little spat yesterday. Yes, I did lunge at Leo when the idiot poured full-cream milk instead of skimmed into my morning coffee. Yes, I did maintain a firm grip round the complainant's neck for longer than is polite. And yes, I did also fire the by-then comatose complainant for sleeping on the job. But I fail to see why my actions are being judged so harshly by the courts and international media at large, since I was not of sound mind when the event took place.

Aries Bastard Boss

TO WHOM IT MAY CONCERN

Leo has a few strange ideas which I am sure would be put to much better use at a more *progressive* company. Perhaps a more *open-minded* boss wouldn't take offense at being called a stubborn old fart. Perhaps a *more economically* with-it boss might feel compelled to agree that it would indeed be *innovative* and *revolutionary* to pay employees in dollars and cents rather than the trusty old pound and shilling.

Taurus Bastard Boss

TO WHOM IT MAY CONCERN

I wish Capricorn every success in the future.

Gemini Bastard Boss

TO WHOM IT MAY CONCERN

Despite a few silly misunderstandings initially—like when this employee mistook my "At this rate, you'll be sitting in my chair within three months," for "At this rate, you'll be sitting in my chair within three months"—Leo never bore me any grudges, which is more than I can say for myself, particularly when, within three months, this employee callously sat in my chair and proceeded to do my job when I was in the bathroom having another personal crisis.

Cancer Bastard Boss

TO WHOM IT MAY CONCERN

Leo is extremely hardworking, stupendously loyal, incredibly talented, massively popular, and stunningly attractive. Unfortunately there was only room for one person like this in my organization.

Leo Bastard Boss

TO WHOM IT MAY CONCERN

Leo worked under my employ from 9:01 P.M., Monday, March 10, 2002[4] to 9:08 A.M., Monday, March 10, 2002.

---

[4] Yes, it was a Monday. Now do shut up, Virgo, and stop interrupting.

Although arriving late to work and leaving early is a sack-able offense in this company, I am prepared to give Leo a second chance as there is still an awful lot of filing left to be done.

Virgo Bastard Boss

TO WHOM IT MAY CONCERN

I have been assured that Leo was a brilliant and conscien-tious employee who ran this corporation without any guid-ance or assistance from me. I have also been informed that there is a direct correlation between Leo leaving and this corporation's consequent collapse.

Executive Personal Assistant on behalf of
Libra Bastard Boss (Receivers Appointed)

TO WHOM IT MAY CONCERN

After just 15 years of service with my company, Leo has decided to move on to new and fresh opportunities. While I am perfectly capable of overlooking such a bla-tant act of treachery and betrayal, I couldn't help but notice two black pens, one blue one, a roll of Scotch Tape and four self-adhesive envelopes also left the office at about the same time, and thus I have no option but to put out a contract on this employee's life.

Scorpio Bastard Boss

TO WHOM IT MAY CONCERN

It was with great sadness that I had to say goodbye to Leo—but anyone who uses the compulsory team-building weekend to organize an insurrection against me in order to ensure our mandatory lunchtime white-water rollerblading sessions are banned for all time, is clearly not very sporting and has no place in this company.

Sagittarius Bastard Boss

TO WHOM IT MAY CONCERN

I must say, Leo certainly livened up the office. Particularly my office. The one at the end of the corridor with views of the city. The one in which I sit all day as head of the company, but Leo never noticed because I tend to blend into the furniture. This oversight would have been forgivable perhaps had Leo been related by marriage to the company-owner's son. Unfortunately Leo is not. I am.

Capricorn Bastard Boss

TO WHOM IT MAY CONCERN

I would like to take this opportunity to point out that accusations of unfair dismissal by this employee are inaccurate and biased, as Leo was neither black, female nor physically or mentally handicapped when sacked for demanding a company car despite the fact the office bike was in perfectly good working order.

Aquarius Bastard Boss

TO WHOM IT MAY CONCERN

By the time you read this, I will no longer be on this earth. Please let the auditors know that it was all Leo's fault.

Pisces Bastard Boss (Morticians Appointed)

THE VIRGO SLAVE

August 24–September 23

MEMO

YOUR REF: AQ BOSS EX VIRG EMPLOYEE/212/B45/HOYYFARTYIOIMN-HJKVDXOO

Dear Aquarius Bastard Boss,

1.1. Thanks for your questions re: the proposed publicity campaign devised by Flashy Oddjob Fawning & Rood. The information you requested is as follows:

* The proposed 45 eight-sheet billboard posters have a biomass roughly equivalent to 1:32 mature trees. That's *Pinus radiata,* not one of the exotic species.

✳ Yes. This is well within national forestry strategy targets.

✳ Yes. The paper will be recycled stuff, and, therefore, no, your consent will in no way result in the eviction of even a single baby squirrel. Making amends by sacrificing a goat to the Earth Goddess is therefore not necessary.

✳

MEMO

YOUR REF: TAU BOSS EX VIRGO EMPLOYEE/254/B64/NOBODYEVERREADS-THISBIT

Dear Taurus Bastard Boss,

✳ I agree. There *is* no future in all this recycled nonsense.

✳ There is, however, a lot of *past.*

✳ No. They *don't* make advertising posters like they used to.

✳

MEMO

YOUR REF: GEM BOSS EX VIRGO EMPLOYEE/245/B62/2B/ORNOT/2B/WHATWASTHEQUESTION

Dear Gemini Bastard Boss,

✳ Yes. You are correct. Due to an administrative oversight, you *were* the only one of the 12 Bastard Department Heads not to receive a copy of the advertising plan. I will send it to you immediately.

✳ In the meantime, I am glad to hear you agree with all of it.

MEMO

YOUR REF: SCO BOSS EX VIRGO EMPLOYEE/254/B79/TALKSLIKE-DENIRO/LOOKSLIKEJOEPESCI

Dear Scorpio Bastard Boss,

The market research results you asked for, re: the advertising slogan:

* 39 people preferred **Our Product Is Really Good**;
* 59 people preferred **Our Product Is Better Than The Others**;
* Only two people preferred **Buy Our Product Or Sam And Gino Will Pay You A Visit And Hit You Across The Knees With A Sock Full Of Billiard Balls**. True, this represented a 100 percent positive response among survey respondents called Sam and Gino, but perhaps we should be careful of catering just to niche markets.
* Even if they *are* your cousins.

✳

MEMO

YOUR REF: PIS BOSS EX VIRGO EMPLOYEE/254/B82/ASHTRAYONA-
MOTORBIKE

Dear Pisces Bastard Boss,

Thank you for your kind and helpful suggestions, all 212 of
them. I've referred them to the advertising agency, and they've
come back with the following replies:

* Suggestions 001—208: **No.**
* Suggestions 209—210: **You must be joking**.
* Suggestion 211: **Hee hee hee hee hee hee hee hee hee hee
  hee hee. Oh stop it. Get out of here. You're cracking me up.
  Ho ho ho ho ho ho ho. Snort snort**.
* Suggestion 212: **Yes. Excellent idea. Pepperidge Farm
  Cookies** *would* **be a lot better than Chips Ahoy at the next
  meeting**.
* Well done. I need hardly tell you, I'm sure, that this is your
  best result ever!

✳

MEMO

YOUR REF: SAG BOSS EX VIRGO EMPLOYEE/254/B50/
QUICKMARCHYOUNASTYLITTLEMEN/LEF-RY-LEF-RY-LEF-RY/HUP:234/
HUP:234

Dear Sagittarius Bastard Boss,
Re: The major prize in the proposed "Buy Our Product And Get A Life" competition.

✶ A recent study at Columbia University sought to identify the main factors influencing consumer habits. The study found that 98.3 percent of people will choose not to buy a particular product if they associate it with:
—extreme terror
—vomiting
—potentially life-threatening injuries
—being suspended upside down above a river full of piranhas
—dislocated ankles

This might suggest, I think, that the company should stick with the idea of a candlelit dinner for two at a nice restaurant. Not everyone, it seems, is as keen on bungee jumping holidays in the Amazon as you are.

✶

MEMO

Dear Virgo Bastard Boss,

Thank you for your very detailed list of questions. The answers are as follows:

✳ $17 \times \{4 - 6n\}^3 + 89.6 > 45$ [y − x = n] − 90, with a statistical variance of less than, or equal to, 0.2 percent.

✳   Tadpoles, unless the alloy contains zinc. In which case, blue.

✳   "Alas, poor Yorrick, I knew him, Horatio."

✳   Madrid, 1954.

I hope that helps with your *Trivial Pursuit* game. If you have any queries about the advertising campaign, please get back to me.

✳

MEMO

YOUR REF: LIB BOSS EX VIRGO EMPLOYEE/245/B72/MIRRORMIRRORON-THEWALL/WHO'STHEBLONDESTOFTHEMALL

Dear Libra Bastard Boss,

I sent on to the advertising agency your comments re: the proposed color scheme to be used on the billboards, as you asked. The agency's replies:

*   Most people are unlikely to react as negatively as you to that precise tone of lemon yellow. Most people did not buy a suit in that color in 1986 only to find that the stitching in the left armpit unravelled after three washings.
*   Your house will be three kilometers from the nearest billboard site. The "pukey pastel blue," as you put it, therefore, will not clash with the mauve of your roof tiles.
*   Leopard-skin was *last* year. Don't you know *anything*?

✳

MEMO

YOUR REF: CAP BOSS EX VIRGO EMPLOYEE/245/B12/YOUNG/GIFTED/
ANDBEIGE

Dear Capricorn Bastard Boss,

Regrettably, not all your questions can be answered at this point. The Freedom of Information legislation is complex. So far, though, I can tell you this:

* Yes. The Fawning in Flashy Oddjob Fawning & Rood *is* related to Judge Fawning of the District Court.
* No, he is not married.
* Yes, a woman called Sonja Marie Betwitz, travel consultant.
* Not really. Once, maybe twice, each week, but she never stays over and hasn't been introduced to His Honor.
* The photographs reveal nothing unusual, although they did try it with cream and jelly once.
* The Mobile Phone Winebar, half a block from the agency, every Friday night from about 6 P.M. Third table from the door on the left. He responds best to miniskirts and Harvey Wallbangers.

✳

MEMO

YOUR REF: CAN BOSS EX VIRGO EMPLOYEE/245/B65/SMILEYOUGRUMPY-
OLDBASTARD

Dear Cancer Bastard Boss,
I appreciate your concerns about the publicity campaign. After exhaustive research, I've come up with the following answers to your detailed questions.

a/ Yes.

b/ Yes.

c/ No.

d/ Yes.

e/ Yes, but . . .

f/ As I was saying . . .

g/ Now, there's no need to . . .

h/ Look at me when I'm talking to you.

i/ *Look* at me.

j/ Well, take the paper bag *off* your head and look at me.

k/ You *do* that then. See if I care.

*

MEMO

Dear Aries Bastard Boss,

Don't hit me, please, but I asked Flashy Oddjob Fawning &
Rood why they rejected your offer to assist with the market
research process. They told me that they did so for two reasons:

Your offer to help—or, as they put it, "help"—consisted of
supplying them, at gunpoint, with 200 names and phone numbers, half of which turned out to be yours. The other half
turned out to be your relations.

A test survey on the first 30 of these people found all of
them, strangely, strongly in favor of using very bright colors on
the billboards, so that, they said, deaf people could understand
them more easily. Curiously enough, noted the agency, this was
one of your ideas—or, as they put it, "ideas."

✳

MEMO

YOUR REF: LEO BOSS EX VIRGO EMPLOYEE/245/B61/APPALLINGOLDLUVVIE

Dear Leo Bastard Boss,

The survey into which celebrity would be best to feature in the television commercials is now complete. The names and their percentage approval ratings are listed below.

Catherine Zeta-Jones: 86 percent

Brad Pitt: 75 percent

Denzel Washington: 71 percent

Britney Spears: 69 percent

The One With The Shortest Skirt From Destiny's Child: 68 percent

You doing Greta Garbo: 0.01 percent

I realize this must be disappointing for you, but you might gain some comfort from knowing that you scored better than the *real* Greta Garbo. She scored just 0.0001 percent, with a staggering 99.9999 percent of people saying that, since she died, she is nowhere *near* as sexy as she used to be. Several people liked your cleavage, by the way, and only three people (way down on last time) suggested that you need either treatment or incarceration.

THE LIBRA SLAVE

September 24–October 23

Known among your peers as the biggest suck this side of Bill Clinton's trousers, you are well-versed in the art of circumnavigating tricky bosses and their even trickier questions—particularly the ridiculous multiple choice ones you're now faced with for the benefit of some hare-brained personnel officers.

1. If you were late for an important client meeting with your **Aries Bastard Boss**, you would:

a) beat him to the punch and resign on the spot;

b) blame it on the one-hour dry-cleaners who left you waiting three hours for your Armani suit;

c) play on his compassionate side by telling him your grandmother died, your dog got run over in a tragic gardening accident, and you've just been told by your doctor that you've got one week to live—then wait to be sacked.

2. After your **Taurus Bastard Boss** hauls you into his office and says he thinks you're indecisive and flighty, you retaliate by saying:

a) D'you really think so? I can leave if you like.

b) Well, at least I don't buy my clothes from K-Mart.

c) Could you please keep your mouth closed when you're eating.

3. Your **Gemini Bastard Boss** keeps forgetting he's got demanding responsibilities, and tends to disappear from the office for hours at a time. Do you:

a) present him with a copy of his job description each and every one of the mornings he bothers to show up;

b) enlist the services of the company's security guards and get him placed under house arrest;

c) silently thank God he's never around, because that Dolce & Gabbana polka dot-check-stripe-plaid suit he likes to wear offends your aesthetic sensibilities.

4. When your **Cancer Bastard Boss** says something that is not particularly funny and obviously expects you to laugh, you:

a) make a strange sort of noncommittal gurgling noise to keep him happy;

b) roll around the floor in genuine hilarity because you think the thought of a Cancer boss attempting humor is hysterical;

c) silently thank God you're a deaf person who's been placed on work experience by a Careers for the Disadvantaged government scheme.

5. At the end of your tether because your **Leo Bastard Boss** is sending you on yet another menial errand, you:

a) point out that, as the marketing manager, it seems a waste of company time and money for you to be scouring hardware stores for a light bulb to replace the one above the mirror in her office;

b) also point out that her three personal stylists are doing nothing but playing computer games right as you speak;

c) do the errand anyway because, as usual, she's too busy taking Polaroids of herself to listen.

6. If you worked for a **Virgo Bastard Boss** you would:

a) kill yourself;

b) kill him;

c) kill him again.

7. In the twilight weeks of a brand new company that your **Libra Bastard Boss** has managed to systematically but by no means deliberately destroy, do you:

a) stand by him because he's the same star sign as you;

b) stand in front of him because he's standing behind you to shield himself from irate employees who are all about to lose their jobs through no fault of their own;

c) stand away from him because you've both turned up wearing identical Prada shirts.

8. You're in the office of your **Scorpio Bastard Boss**, busily
dusting the executive toys on his desk. Suddenly he's behind
you. Do you:

a) emit a blood-curdling scream;
b) quietly fart;
c) ignore him as you're used to him following you around to
   ensure you're not pocketing his paperweights.

9. You find your **Sagittarius Bastard Boss** in tears because
everyone's been rolling their eyes at his trite aphorisms and
unclever clichés. Do you:

a) resist the urge to say, "I'm not going to say I told you so," and
   instead console him with, "Don't worry. Those who laugh
   last, laugh longest."
b) refuse to feel sorry for him—he's a Sagittarian and therefore had it coming;
c) try to be fair-minded and yell: "*You're* upset? How d'you
   think all the poor schmucks who have to *listen* to you feel?"

10. For the third time this week, your **Capricorn Bastard Boss**
arrives at work dressed in brown and beige from head to toe.
Do you:

a) go home sick;
b) hope in vain he's being ironic;

c) think, "Oh, well, at least he's stopped parting his hair down the middle."

11. When you turn up to the office in your brand new sealskin shoes, do you notice your **Aquarius Bastard Boss** looking a bit upset?

a) kind of;

b) um, no, not really;

c) upset about what? They're only made from baby seals, for God's sake, not endangered species!

12. Your **Pisces Bastard Boss** has taken time off to have a nervous breakdown and asks you to hold the fort. Do you:

a) have a nervous breakdown yourself;

b) tell him to grow up, get a grip and stop doing so many drugs;

c) wonder why a Piscean was given so much responsibility in the first place.

Having successfully avoided answering any of the above questions, but nevertheless made a very nice origami owl out of the paper they're printed on, you will no doubt infuriate the personnel officers and hopefully never get invited to apply for a job in a bank or the public service again.

THE SCORPIO SLAVE

October 24–November 22

With a GED in Lurking Patiently Behind Doors, a Bachelor's in Padding Quietly Down Corridors, and a Master's in Keeping Your Mouth Shut For A Price, all gained from the Scorpio School of Thought, you secretly know it's just a matter of time and a fastidiously kept diary before you get the perks, promotions and pay raises you so rightly deserve from all 12 of your bastard bosses.

January:

Catch **Capricorn Bastard Boss** reading my mind. This is unfortunate because I have just been thinking what a complete and utter dickhead he is and if he doesn't increase my salary soon, his well-heeled, well-connected wife is going to find out that the only constructive social climbing he's been doing of late is onto his desk with the incredibly friendly new receptionist.

February:

Catch my **Aquarius Bastard Boss** eating a non-vegetarian burger made from non-free-range cows and slurping coffee ground from a non-politically correct South American republic from a non-environmentally friendly polystyrene cup. Will use it to get non-negotiable, non-refundable pay raise.

March:

While hovering behind the executive door, my **Pisces Bastard Boss** calls me into the corridor and virtually begs me to take his job. Cast him a withering look and tell him I've already got it— which is why I'm the one hovering behind the executive door and he's the one in the corridor.

April:

Snuck into the office to type up my résumé on the weekend only to witness my **Aries Bastard Boss** smiling in a warm and caring sort of way while doling out peanut butter and jelly sand-wiches to a group of children he'd invited in from the local orphanage. The look of horror on my employer's face when he saw me was priceless (as will be my salary cap).

May:

After all his mutterings about getting back to basics and promptly issuing staff with rocks and chisels, I must admit I was slightly taken aback when I spotted my **Taurus Bastard Boss** covertly scratching away on a piece of parchment with a quill.

Feel duty-bound to confiscate them until I get my slate and chalk back.

June:

After noticing my **Gemini Bastard Boss** sneaking out of the office for an important meeting at a nearby video arcade, I chance upon a doctor's report at the bottom of the towering pile of papers in his in-tray. To my surprise, discover that not only is he suffering from attention deficit disorder, multiple personality syndrome, and amnesia, but the poor thing also has herpes. For a small fee and a slightly bigger office, shall offer not to inform his wife. Assuming he remembers he has a wife. Possibly several.

July:

Find my **Cancer Bastard Boss** at it again in the men's toilets, face toward the urinal, shuddering and groaning, and making disgusting ghastly noises whilst wads of damp tissues accumulate at his feet. Wipe all the gunk off the walls, his clothes and his face and promise I won't breathe a word that he's been crying again, of course so long as he approves my expense receipts for the rest of the year.

August:

Receive, and sign for, an express-couriered envelope that is addressed to my **Leo Bastard Boss**. Thinking it contains another fawning piece of fan mail, my boss rips the envelope out of my hand (before I have time to steam it open), reads the contents within, then flops into a fetal position on the floor, wailing loudly. I, in turn, steal a glance at the offending contents and manage to make out that they're actually adoption papers, ones that clearly reveal my boss is not the real son of God, after all. After receiving a business lunch account that could feed the five thousand, I reassure my devastated employer that this shocking secret is safe with me.

September:

My ever-paranoid **Virgo Bastard Boss** has accused me of trying to steal his job. Needless to say, I immediately put it back in the filing cabinet where I found it.

October:

While my **Libra Bastard Boss** was out having his weekly facial, massage and pedicure, I happened across a shopping bag marked "Private & Confidential" sequestered in the double-locked safe behind the door that says "No staff beyond this point." Though I did not have time to thoroughly analyze the contents, I did make out that the three cotton/polyester dry cleanable crew-necked T-shirts were—how humiliating—*off the rack*. Shall tell him I too can be bought—but only at a *haute couture* price.

November:

While I am rifling through the desk of my **Scorpio Bastard Boss** in the dead of night, I spy, through the two-way mirror installed in his office, him rummaging around some drawers in my office next door. He, in turn, spies me through a similar mirror that I have installed in my office. Unfortunately, the incriminating blackmail note addressed to him that he finds in my drawers is nothing compared to the incriminating sex video I find in his.

December:

It seems my **Sagittarius Bastard Boss** does not always adhere to the old adage, *practice what you preach*. Upon overhearing that he lost his house, children, and pets in a tragic gardening accident after his wife sued for divorce on the grounds of extreme neglect because he was always away on staff bonding courses, I felt compelled to offer my commiserations. My cheery, heartfelt, "buck up, boy, it can't be all that bad, let's go for a therapeutic rock climb," was met with a very unsporting punch in the solar plexus. Will give him one back if he doesn't foot my medical expenses.

THE SAGITTARIUS SLAVE

November 23–December 21

Never one to be tied down to one job for too long, you've decided you had better update your *curriculum vitae* in preparation for the next one. Believing, as archers always do, that honesty is the best policy, you list the dozen previous bastard bosses you worked for, the ridiculous tasks they made you carry out, and your very good reasons for leaving 12 jobs in as many hours.

COMPLETE BASTARDS INC
Worked for **Aries Bastard Boss.**
Official Title   *"Oi, you!"*
Job Description   *Licking my employer's boots clean and then doing 1000 push-ups for doing the former task improperly.*
Reason for Leaving   *Unable to do 1000 push-ups due to having both arms hacked off with a machete during heated, albeit muffled, altercation with boss over how the hell I was supposed to be able to lick his boots when he refused to take the gaffer tape off my mouth.*

*

STUBBORN OLD BASTARD PTY LTD
Worked for **Taurus Bastard Boss.**
Official Title   *"Secretary" (or, what I would prefer to term, "Personal Assistant")*
Job Description   *Trying to convince the stubborn old bastard that no one uses the word "secretary" anymore, continually thumping my fist on my manual typewriter to make my point.*
Reason for Leaving   *Repetitive Strain Injury (or, as my boss termed it, "You Can't Get Good Help These Days").*

*

BASTARD, BASTARD & BASTARD
Worked for **Gemini Bastard Boss.**
Official Title   *Accountant (or Administrator or Janitor or Clerk or Computer Programmer or Courier or Dispatch Person or Managing Director or Office Manager or Personal Assistant or Receptionist or Zoologist—which one depending very much upon my employer's state of mind at the time).*
Job Description   *Unknown.*
Reason for Leaving   *Felt I was losing my identity.*

✳

UNINTELLIGIBLE BASTARDS R US
Worked for **Cancer Bastard Boss.**
Official Title   *Resident Psychic/Agony Aunt*
Job Description   *Working out what kind of mood my boss would be in each day so I could affect appropriate facial expression of sympathy/compassion/concern when listening to the idiot's tales of terminal woe.*
Reason for Leaving   *Struck the "God, that's awful" pose when I should have struck the "God, that's really awful" one.*

✳

VAIN BASTARD CORPORATION
Worked for **Leo Bastard Boss.**
Official Title   *Public Relations Officer*
Job Description   *Protecting my boss from constructive criticism, unflattering light and bad camera angles while, at the same time, trying to blend discreetly into the few walls that didn't have floor-to-ceiling mirrors.*
Reason for Leaving   *Did neither task very successfully.*

✳

POINTLESS BASTARD & CO
Worked for **Virgo Bastard Boss.**
Official Title   *Assistant Manager*
Job Description   *Monitoring milk, tea, coffee and cookie supplies, conducting stationery stocktakes (including the counting of individual paper clips, staples and rubber bands), collecting and then piecing back together all correspondence from the shredding machine to check that all confidential memos issued from the boss were being shredded as instructed, and then writing detailed hourly reports on findings so boss could be kept informed at all times.*
Reason for Leaving   *See Job Description.*

✳

USELESS BASTARD & USELESS BASTARD'S SON
Worked for **Libra Bastard Boss.**

Official Title   *Office Decorator (Unofficial Title: Managing Director)*

Job Description   *Making successful corporate bids, raids and takeovers, floating company on stock market, conducting annual general meetings, hiring and firing staff, redecorating company offices on a seasonal basis.*

Reason for Leaving   Couldn't get my boss to decide whether he wanted company offices painted blue to match his eyes, green to match his business acumen or red to match his father's face when the latter found out his son had blown shareholder profits on genuine Louis XVI office desks for all 850 members of staff.

✳

SUSPICIOUS BASTARD UNLIMITED
Worked for **Scorpio Bastard Boss.**

Official Title   *Head of Internal Affairs*

Job Description   *Stamping out corruption among the workers.*

Reason for Leaving   Got caught on closed-circuit camera pocketing two Fig Newtons from staff kitchen.

✳

STUPID BASTARD INC
Worked for **Sagittarius Bastard Boss.**

Official Title　*Neuro-Linguistics Officer*

Job Description　*Collecting doctors' certificates, filling in Medicare rebate forms, applying for private health insurance, calling ambulances, filing workers' compensation forms and ordering wreaths for bereaved family members of deceased staff.*

Reason for Leaving　*Unable to carry out duties due to two broken arms, a hernia and a suspected brain lesion acquired after attending, at my employer's request, the three-day "A Healthy Worker is a Wealthy Worker" workshop.*

✳

BORING BEIGE BASTARD & CO
Worked for **Capricorn Bastard Boss.**

Official Title　*Smythe with a "y."*

Job Description　*Trying to hide from my boss the fact that I was actually Smith with an "i," nor was I related to anybody with a double-barrelled surname (not unless you count my uncle, John Shotgun-Smith who recently escaped from jail).*

Reason for Leaving　*Fired from place of work after uncle subsequently robbed it.*

✳

WEIRD BASTARD FOR WORLD PEACE INC
Worked for **Aquarius Bastard Boss.**

Official Title *None because, as I was told by my boss,* ad infinitum, *official titles are fascist conspiracies aimed at subjugating and delineating the masses, thus causing low morale and collective paranoia.*

Job Description *Volunteering to stop work to assist boss in rearrangement of entire office in accordance to latest feng shui trends. Volunteering every other lunchbreak to don a koala suit and collect money for the Wilderness Society, and wasting the other ones disposing of my sandwich wrappers, plastic yogurt cartons and aluminium drink cans in the multitude of specialist recycling bins spread around the office.*

Reason for Leaving *Didn't carry out aforementioned tasks in the appropriate caring way. (And how was I to know the hairy raccoon was endangered? I thought it was a rat.)*

*

PATHETIC BASTARD PTY LTD
Worked for **Pisces Bastard Boss.**

Official Title *Junior Clerk*

Job Description *Taking blame for everything that went wrong in organization, from the rubber plant in the front foyer dying to company share prices falling on the Dow Jones Index.*

Reason for Leaving *Company folded (thanks to me).*

THE CAPRICORN SLAVE

December 22–January 20

Let's do lunch. Your choice.

The memo from the boss was on your desk when you arrived this morning. This could be big, you think. Very big. Promotion. Responsibility. Maybe even an invitation to join the golf club and hang out with all the boss's Mercedes-driving friends. You are a Capricorn. This is irresistible.

But not without hazard. Pick the wrong type of eatery, after all, and the boss could come to the conclusion that you're a boorish philistine and banish you to the Northern Branch Office in some satellite town full of people who wear chain-store clothes and think the Spice Girls are cool. *Your choice*, the memo said. It is, quite clearly, a test.

You are not unduly worried, however. You are a Capricorn, after all, and knowledge, you realize, is power. You know the boss's star sign. All you have to do is consult your handy cut-out-and-keep *Guide To Schmoozing Your Bastard Boss.*

ARIES BASTARD BOSS

Where to eat: Somewhere you'll never want to visit again, given how badly the boss will insult the staff.

What to order: Avoid bread sticks. These have been known to become lethal weapons in the hands of an Aries bastard boss with a point to make.

What to drink: A box of wine. Cardboard boxes can do only superficial damage when flung at a waiter who fails to deliver the entrées speedily enough.

What to talk about: The boss's latest business triumph, upping productivity by a whopping 25 percent simply by connecting all the office chairs to the electricity.

What not to talk about: The hideous and pus-filled blisters on your buttocks.

Useful get-to-the-point conversation starter: "So, enough about you, let's talk about *you.*"

TAURUS BASTARD BOSS

Where to eat: Ronnie's Ribs, The Beefsteak And Bourbon Bar, The Scorched Corpse Bistro, something like that. Taurean bosses like their food plain, solid and hefty. They are suspicious of nouvelle cuisine, despise fancy lettuces, and think tofu is a type of martial art.

What to order: Good, old-fashioned fodder: a meatloaf sandwich, T-bone steak, lambs' fry and bacon, French fries, lashings of tomato sauce. If that's not enough, you can always go back for seconds.

What to drink: The stuff all Taurean bosses like to drink: real ale or stout, served warm and frothing in pints, preferably with bits of weevil and leaf-mold floating on the top of it.

What to talk about: The decline of modern morals, the shiftlessness of youth, the good old days when people had to work or starve, none of this namby-pamby social security nonsense then, National Service, that's what we need. Alternatively, you could just bark a lot.

What not to talk about: The gradual build-up of white froth across the boss's upper lip and nose.

Useful conversation starter: "I notice you've upgraded your mobile phone. That *is* a new piece of string in the end of your baked bean tin, isn't it?"

GEMINI BASTARD BOSS

Where to eat: McDonald's, KFC, Pizza Hut—somewhere where you don't have to wait more than two minutes to be served.

What to order: It doesn't matter really, because the boss will have gone off the idea by the time it arrives. Those kiddy-meal packs which include a free plastic cartoon character might maintain amusement a little longer.

What to drink. Schnapps. Anything that requires more than one gulp to finish will fail to sustain the boss's interest.

What to talk about: Anything you like, really, as long as you remember to change the subject every 30 seconds.

What not to talk about: The fact that you feel having to cut up the boss's Junior Space Hero Tastee-Crust Mini-Pizza and deliver each forkful to the executive gob while making airplane noises falls considerably outside your job description.

Useful get-to-the-point conversation starter: "So, I expect you're wondering why you asked to see me . . ."

CANCER BASTARD BOSS

Where to eat: A dimly lit restaurant with booth seating. That way the boss will feel more secure if sitting under the table in a huff becomes an option.

What to order: Avoid pumpkin soup or enchiladas. Pumpkin soup would remind the boss of the glorious summer spent with Mary, the deceitful cow, in the Scottish highlands. And enchiladas make him fart.

What to drink: Avoid rum, gin, whiskey or anything else likely to bring on the tears. Champagne should lift the spirits, at least until he sees the label and realizes it's exactly what dear Helen was drinking the last time he saw her so many years ago.

What to talk about: Stick to vague generalities such as the weather, although even this could set him off if he remembers that Jane—how he misses her—quite liked weather.

What not to talk about: Anything else.

Useful get-to-the-point conversation starter: "I agree, yes, 13 broken love affairs is an awful burden to bear. Are you interested in dating my sister?"

LEO BASTARD BOSS

Where to eat: Somewhere with a lot of mirrors. Avoid table-top dancing clubs, however, because few Leo bastard bosses can resist the temptation to strip down to undies and show the girls how to *really* shake some ass.

What to order: An irrelevant consideration. The boss will order just to prove to the waiter that he or she can speak French.

You will find that deep-fried geranium wrapped in toupee in a juicy cat sauce can be surprisingly appetizing.

What to drink: So-called "performance-enhancing" drinks: a yard of ale, a dry martini with pimento olive, a Flaming Lamborghini, a Cosmopolitan or a can of beer wedged in the cleavage of the waitress. The choice depends on whether the boss is being Oliver Reed, F. Scott Fitzgerald, Carrie from *Sex and the City*, or Henry VIII.

What to talk about: The boss.

What not to talk about: Yourself. Or Bette Davis (unless you are prepared to listen to the entire dénouement speech from *All About Eve*, complete with costume hastily improvised from the tablecloth and the two halves of cantaloupe on the fresh fruit and cheese platter).

Useful get-to-the-point conversation starter: "So, what's a gorgeous creature like you doing in a place like this?"

VIRGO BASTARD BOSS

Where to eat: An Internet cafe—one of those places which serve every main meal with a side order of database and a meticulously detailed bill.

What to order: A complete inventory of the kitchen stock and an audit of the last two years of accounts. It would be politic to let the Virgo boss double-check your figures.

What to drink: Every now and then, a liquor company does a promotion whereby if you drink six glasses of their product you win a free T-shirt. They give you a little form to fill out so you can keep track of your progress. Virgo bastard bosses love these.

What to talk about: New developments in accounting procedures, or the sexy new range of ring-binder files just in the shops.

What not to talk about. The boss's health. You'll never hear the end of it. It would also be impolite to ask why he or she appears to be recording your conversation on a dictaphone and taking minutes on the back of the napkin.

Useful get-to-the-point conversation starter: "Did you know that the chap who invented double-entry bookkeeping is an acquaintance of mine?"

LIBRA BASTARD BOSS

Where to eat: A very stylish, ultra-modern trattoria situated midway between a major television studio and a modeling agency.

What to order: Soufflé and sorbet: the precise flavors will depend on the decor.

What to drink: Galliano. Tell the boss that Dior swears by it.

What to talk about: Nothing that ends with a question mark.

And nothing too difficult. The cut of the executive shirt—with special reference to the logo—would be a good tack.

What not to talk about: The Big Four: business, politics, religion, off-the-rack clothing.

Useful get-to-the-point conversation starter: "Did you know that Coco Chanel was a friend of my mother?"

SCORPIO BASTARD BOSS

Where to eat: Big Joey's Pasta Palace, Uncle Gino's Bella Ristorante, or one of the several other establishments run by his curiously fawning "business associates."

What to order: Whatever the boss wants, and quickly. It is also good manners to ask the boss if he'd like to shoot the waiter in the foot.

What to drink: Red wine. The special stuff in the cellar. Tell the waiter to hop to it.

What to talk about: The good old days. The numbers game (hint: this is not *The Price Is Right*). The fact that your sister, at 34, is still a virgin. Your mother, too.

What not to talk about: The thing that appears to be a dead mouse in the boss's mouth. It's just one of his wodges of cotton wool slipped a bit.

Useful get-to-the-point conversation starter: "Did you know my father went into business with John Gotti? He developed a new ammunition storage container, called the back of his head."

SAGITTARIUS BASTARD BOSS

Where to eat: The Saddle-Pack Dude Ranch out in the country: the place that lets you mount a horse and lasso your own cow before you order the steak.

What to order: Steak, of course. No self-respecting Sagittarius bastard boss will want to waste time lassoing sheep or chickens.

What to drink: Glucose-heavy sports drinks. You can't jog around the dining room between courses *drunk*, can you?

What to talk about: How well the boss handled the lasso, and, yes, how truly difficult it is, when doing a flat-out gallop, to distinguish between a Poll Hereford steer and a six-year-old girl on a Shetland pony.

What not to talk about: The fact that you just found what appears to be a small tuft of mane in your porterhouse.

Useful get-to-the-point conversation starter: "Did you know my brother's business never really took off until he decided to climb Mount Everest with one hand tied behind his back?"

CAPRICORN BASTARD BOSS

Where to eat: A private club, the exclusive domain of the rich and powerful. (Being a Capricorn, you will of course know someone who works there who can swing the invitation.)

What to order: Whatever the bishop at the next table is having.

What to drink: *Not* what the bishop is having. Sacramental wine tastes horrible until you get used to it.

What to talk about: It doesn't matter. The boss will be too busy eavesdropping on the other diners to pay attention to *you*.

What not to talk about: Fog. There's no need to be personal, after all.

Useful get-to-the-point conversation starter: "I see we have the same hairstyle. We center-partings have to stick together, don't we?"

AQUARIUS BASTARD BOSS

Where to eat: The Soul Food Macrobiotic Vegan Organic Health Brasserie And Vedic Meditation Center.

What to order: Whatever you want. Lumpy pale brown mush is lumpy pale brown mush, no matter what you call it.

What to drink: The house speciality: runny pale brown mush.

What to talk about: Chakras, if you can manage it. If not, just beat the table and perform a Native American healing chant.

What not to talk about: The mixed grill you enjoyed at your hunting lodge yesterday.

Useful get-to-the-point conversation starter: "I see a statue of Buddha over there. He was a friend of my uncle, you know."

PISCES BASTARD BOSS

Where to eat: An American diner, where the staff whiz about on roller skates. At least then when he tries to give them a hand you can have a good laugh.

What to order: You will not order. The boss will order for you, just to feel useful. Hope you like nachos topped with pineapple fritters.

What to drink: As much as you can. You'll need it.

What to talk about: Why the two of you appear to be standing in the restaurant kitchen washing up, doing a fine job of not impressing the chef.

What not to talk about: The fact that the executive elbow is currently resting in a bowl of leftover chicken and sweetcorn soup.

Useful get-to-the-point conversation starter: "I'd love to lend you $50 to settle the bill, but you haven't actually paid me yet."

THE AQUARIUS SLAVE

January 21–February 19

Dear Bastard Bosses,

Blessings to you all. I am pleased to present my survey on employee–employer relations, as you requested. I apologize for its late delivery, but it took me ages to find suitable recycled paper to put through the photocopier. (I made it myself in the end. If you put it in a flowerpot and water it when you've finished reading, the alfalfa sprouts should take root nicely.) Here goes, then:

Aries Bastard Boss. *Try not to shout at your staff so much: it disturbs the inner harmony of the office. Giving each of them 15 minutes off every day for lunch might be a good idea, particularly if you encourage them to eat macrobiotic vegan food. You might also consider* *unshackling them from their desks, and asking the big guy near the door with the war drum to smile every now and then.*

Taurus Bastard Boss. *I know you don't believe he exists, but my channelling spirit, Chief Widdling Buffalo, feels strongly that you should modernize a bit. In particular he feels that your data entry staff would be a lot happier if you connected their computers to the electricity system. He says quite a lot of businesses do that sort of thing nowadays, and, anyway, forcing that poor donkey to walk round and round in circles all day is never going to generate enough power to work the Pentium processors.*

Gemini Bastard Boss. *It is good for the soul to be relaxed in the work environment, but do you think that slinging a hammock above your desk sends the wrong message? Perhaps try meditation instead. That way you'll still look like you're doing something. Also, some of your employees feel you don't pay enough attention when they're trying to explain things to . . . Hello? Excuse me . . . Oh, never mind.*

Cancer Bastard Boss. *I'm sorry if this report offended you, and perhaps when you unlock the bathroom door and come out again we can discuss it. In the meantime, I know a little place which sells herbal Prozac. I'll give you the address, if you like.*

Leo Bastard Boss. *Your decision to take up Buddhism was a good one, but many of your employees seem disturbed by your new habit of walking around the office in saffron robes and proclaiming yourself to be the Dalai Lama. The real Dalai Lama, they know, isn't at all inter-*

ested in selling build-it-yourself Ezee-Swim pool and sauna kits. Your idea to display a photograph and plaque for the "Worker Of The Month" was also a step in the right direction, but you might try awarding the honor to someone other than yourself once in a while.

Virgo Bastard Boss. *Lighten up! Let your chakras run free. Try to make yourself seem more human to your staff. Your attempt to get into the* Guinness Book Of Records *was certainly a step in the right direction, but next time, perhaps, try something a bit more, well,* fun. *The workers, I'm sure, didn't even realize there* was *a world record for marathon buttock-clenching. Also try for a bit more give-and-take. The staff giving you a cake for your birthday was a good sign. Making them fill out requisition slips before they could eat a piece of it was not.*

Libra Bastard Boss. *I agree with you that color therapy is important, but some of your staff feel that repainting the office each month to match the front cover of* Better Homes And Gardens *is just a tad disruptive. They also feel you should show a little more leadership. Your last memo to them, pointing out that lime green and orange were* last *season's colors, was appreciated, but they felt it failed to address their real concerns, which can be easily summarized: What are they supposed to be* doing *all day?*

Scorpio Bastard Boss. *I know you think your employees are all happy, but quite a number of them actually resent having to kickback 10 percent of their wages to you as protection money. Also, shooting that nice man from the union was inadvisable, karma-wise. I'm glad you took up my earlier suggestion of lighting incense sticks in the office, but* *forcing them under the fingernails of your secretary first was perhaps counterproductive. Thank you, too, for the horse's head you sent me. I'm sending it back, though, because I'm a vegetarian and, anyway, it's starting to smell a bit. Hope you don't mind.*

Sagittarius Bastard Boss. *Your employees tell me that they all thoroughly enjoyed the recent motivational bush survival weekend you organized for them—something I'm sure they'll tell you themselves just as soon as the hospital discharges them. Uniting the mind and body is a worthy aim, but perhaps weekly tai chi sessions in place of your daily unarmed combat workouts might improve morale and decrease your sick-pay blow-out. In the meantime, your decision to make the office more wheelchair-accessible was farsighted and will no doubt be appreciated more and more by the staff as time goes on.*

Capricorn Bastard Boss. *You have a visibility problem among your employees (not, of course, that this will worry you). When shown photographs, almost half your staff could not distinguish between you and the coffee stain on the carpet near the filing cabinet. The rest thought you were rising damp. You already know this, of course. Your recent guest appearance on* The X Files *went over well with the workers. They were as upset as you, I'm sure, to find out that Gillian Anderson thought you were computer generated.*

Aquarius Bastard Boss. *Many of your staff, I'm sad to say, think your latest innovation (rather admirable, to my mind) has led to considerable overcrowding in the workplace. If they don't stop grumbling soon, perhaps you should consider moving the dolphin tank outside into the* corridor. *Your kind gift to each employee of a hand-crafted terracotta oil-burner was appreciated, because at least they covered the smell of dead mackerel. Many of the staff, however, say that burning patchouli is not what they need to make them work better. Perhaps you should try giving them money as well.*

Pisces Bastard Boss. *I know where you're coming from, but putting fish-hooks through your nipples and hanging by them from the ceiling every time you don't meet your sales target is making your workers feel edgy. Try to accept adversity in a more practical manner—by doing some work, perhaps. On a positive note, your people really do appreciate your frequent offers to help them with their daily tasks, but would possibly be more likely to accept your assistance if you didn't ask them to spank you with a ping-pong bat every time you make a trifling mistake.*

Hari Krishna Hari Rama Hari Hari.

Yours sincerely,

The Aquarius Employee.

THE PISCES SLAVE

February 20–March 20

"Well, I've looked everywhere," huffs **Cancer Bastard Boss**. "*My Generation*, by The Who. Can't find it. I've looked under T, and W, and M, and G. It's not there. It's not fair."

You look up and sigh. No imagination, these people; no feeling for the plainly obvious. "Have you checked under S?" you ask. Cancer looks at you, hurt and suspicious. "For Sixties," you explain.

You are beginning to regret this job. Head Librarian for the Megacorp Music Broadcasting Network sounded good at the time, but that was before you realized the 12 bastard boss programmers would be popping in every day, looking for this or that song, actually wanting to *use* the place. And failing miserably in their quests.

After all, it took you three *months* to design out the filing system. By the time you finished, it was so easy to use that even a blind man could do it. As long as his guide dog could read and remembered the label, cover design and approximate release date of Bruce Springsteen's *Born To Run*. But, no, the bastards had been popping in there ever since, asking ridiculous questions, interrupting your continued reading of *The Celestine Prophesy* and your contemplation of the vase of gerberas you keep on the windowsill. Like now.

"Gilbert and Sullivan. The one that begins, 'I am the very model of a modern major general.'" Lots of syllables. Very complicated. Has to be **Virgo Bastard Boss**. "Under M," you say, patiently. "For Military music."

Virgo notes that down in his electronic organizer and moves off, just getting out of the way before **Sagittarius Bastard Boss** bounds in, ruddy of cheek, and bereft of ideas, miming and quoting *The Rocky Horror Show*.

You have to stop him before he gets to the bit about pelvic thrusts. The gerberas are in danger. "It's called 'Time Warp,'" you explain. "You'll find it under H."

"Why?" comes the question. You close your eyes. All that work. Could it be any easier, really? "H," you say, "for Had A Midget In The Film Clip."

Next comes **Aquarius Bastard Boss**. "I've just seen that," he says, "while I was looking for the soundtrack to *Hair*." You tell him it's under N. "I get it," says Aquarius, fiddling with his Native American pendant, "N for Nudie Bits." "No," you reply. "N for Not Very Good."

He blesses you and leaves. You are no more than two pages farther on when you feel a strange, unpleasant chill in the air. You look up and around. Nothing, just a patch of low cloud above the photocopier. "Good morning, **Capricorn Bastard Boss**," you manage.

"I need a new theme tune," she says. "I was thinking of 'God Save The Queen.'"

"Try under S," you say.

"I knew that," she says, departing. "S for Stand Up When You Hear This."

It was S for Sex Pistols, actually. You can't resist laughing, so it's probably a good thing that you don't feel like doing so. Laughter, anyway, would be unwise with **Aries Bastard Boss** now entering the room.

"Give me my song!" he demands. "'I Am, I Said,' by Neil Diamond. I can't find it."

You're about to tell him it's under A, for Almost Worn Out, or Aries' Favorite Song, take your pick, when he interrupts you. "Never mind," he says, "I'll record my own version. I'm much better at it, after all."

Taurus Bastard Boss stomps in. "Can't be doing with all this modern music," he says. "Can't be doing with these new-fangled compact disc players. By the time you've cut the record down to size, there's only the label left. Where have all the wax cylinders gone?" This could be trouble, you realize. You melted them last week. Well, they *looked* like candles. You have an idea.

"Check in the computer database," you say. He leaves immediately, muttering something about an abacus being good enough in his day.

There is to be no peace, however. **Scorpio Bastard Boss** has just arrived. He doesn't even get a chance to open his mouth. "Theme from *The Godfather*," you say. "Under B for Marlon Brando."

"What else is under Marlon Brando?" he asks.

"A broken chair, more often than not," you reply. At that moment, **Libra Bastard Boss** prances in, looking the spitting image of David Bowie doing Ziggy Stardust. "Destiny's Child!" he squeals. You hand him a piece of paper. "Is this the classification number?" he asks.

"No," you reply. "It's the telephone number of a psychiatrist I know. Try over there."

"Under what?" he asks.

"The right hand leg of that wobbly shelving unit," you reply.

He doesn't understand, poor lamb. Nothing new there. Nothing new with **Leo Bastard Boss**, either, who's just come swanning through, humming the big number from *Sunset Boulevard*, complete with arm movements. "Ask me if I know your mother," he prompts. Again.

You grit your teeth, and do so. "No," he yells, *"But if you hum the introduction I might recognize the tune!"*

You hit the canned laughter you keep in a cassette recorder for just such occasions. Leo smiles—just like he always does—bows, weeps a little, bows again, clutches your gerberas to his heaving bosom, thanks you, bows again, and sweeps off, stage left.

Which leaves **Pisces Bastard Boss**. You're surprised. He's usually been in by now, tripping over things, and looking for "You Got A Friend," James Taylor (under V, for Vaguely Nauseating), "Nobody Does It Better" by Carly Simon (under S for Sickly Sweet), or "We Didn't Start The Fire," Billy Joel (also S, for Stop, Stop, Turn it off, Pleeeeeaaassee). So far, no sign. You smile. Maybe you will get a little peace and quiet, after all.

The telephone rings. It's him. Pisces.

"I've just been helping the trainee radio announcers, and they've made lots of mistakes," he tells you. "Do you know how I can get my necktie unwound from reel-to-reel tape decks?"

You contemplate for a moment putting on a funny accent and pretending to be an Indian restaurant. Then you have a better idea. "Yes," you say, "but I'll need a bunch of gerberas."

✧ ABOUT THE AUTHORS ✧

ADÈLE LANG is the author of four books, including the *New York Times* bestselling novel, *Confessions of a Sociopathic Social Climber*. Her books have recently been published in the United States, the U.K., Italy, France, Germany, Korea, Poland, and Australia. She spends most of her working day procrastinating about writing her next novel.

ANDREW MASTERSON is the author of several books, published in the United States, the U.K., Italy, and Australia. He is also a moderately prolific journalist. When he is not writing or researching, he is generally drinking. Recently commissioned to write a book about beer, he is approaching bliss.